NEEDLEPOINT
FOR THE HOME

ANN ELLIS

NEEDLEPOINT FOR THE HOME

ANN ELLIS

B. T. Batsford Ltd, London

Designs by Ann Ellis
Graphics by Jane Tidswell
Photographs by Paul Barker, Ian Wren, Ann Ellis

Typeset by Lasertext Ltd., Stretford, Manchester
and printed in Hong Kong

Published by B. T. Batsford Ltd
4 Fitzhardinge Street, London W1H 0AH

A catalogue record for this book is available from the
British Library

ISBN 0 7134 6545 X

CONTENTS

ACKNOWLEDGEMENTS

So many people were involved during the preparation of this book. Some, like my family, may feel that they were taken for granted, but many willingly gave their time and expertise without knowing how important it was to my peace of mind.

I could not have put this book together without constant support and practical help from Jane Tidswell, who persists in considering everyone else's needs before her own. Her artistic skills extended from the graphics, the sewing and the arranging of photographic sets, to straightforward clearing-up after everyone. I am indebted to her.

Mathew Warwick made me a beautiful walnut frame with African blackwood fittings. He designed it to fit my working methods and it has helped enormously in the completion of much of my work. Although I keep many pieces of work on a variety of frames, there was some juggling done in order to transfer the favoured canvas onto the frame. I have evolved a manner of working that enables me to sew for long periods which I wanted to pass on. I am grateful for the professional advice of Louise Davies and information about posture that is important for all of us.

Antonia Graham, Mrs Shand Kydd and Mr Quinn lent items from their shops for the illustrations. Anthony Bryant, Philip Brown, Jenny Edmonds and Julie Arkell have permitted me to reproduce pictures of their work. John and Joan Packard lent the dolls' house furniture, which provided some entertaining moments and a much-needed break in a busy schedule as the photographer put the 'set' together.

Most of the items were worked for the book, but I did borrow the 'frivolous cushion'. Now owned by Gilly German, she must have thought it had a built-in homing device as she returned it for photography, charting and then colour coding. My thanks for the continuous loan and for her infectious enthusiasm for fabrics and interiors.

Caroline Redmond upholstered the big chair, seat cushion and stool top; each had its individual problem and an imposed deadline. I have appreciated the high standard of her work and her interest in the whole project. John and Dena Bower used their skills to make the stool base and to line the sewing tray. It is to their credit that, despite a very limited brief, each item was just what I was looking for. Pat White and her staff were most helpful in producing the instructions for tassels so that everyone can understand them. Tassels are rather like an elephant – more easily recognized than described – but the instructions given here have been 'test driven'. Pat also used her valuable time to make the feather box to perfection – the work of a true friend.

My thanks to Mr Brown of H. W. Peel & Co., who understood our form of graphics and supplied just what we needed; also to Coats Leisure Crafts for giving me 394 colours to play with, and to Alison Bell for producing the rainbow silk to illustrate a technique.

Thanks also to Kate Harris for her touch with arranging objects and finding just what was needed, and to Susie Edwards whose talents ranged from providing flowers to finding a window for the pelmet design. Ian Wren and Paul Barker showed saintly tolerance, not only with textile photography, but also to working with a complete novice. How their skills reproduced my personal images still seems like magic to me. Their interest and care has been much appreciated.

COLOUR PHOTOGRAPHY CREDITS

Paul Barker was responsible for all location photography as seen on pages 8, 9, 12, 17, 26, 40, 49, 50, 56, 61, 64, 70, 79, 87, 90, 91, 102, 118, 124 and 133. Ian Wren was responsible for the studio photography as seen on pages 15, 21, 31, 33, 35, 38, 39, 44, 51, 53, 59, 63, 75, 76, 84, 94, 98, 107, 108, 110, 112, 114, 119, 122, 123, 129, 130, 132, 134 and 137. The photograph on page 120 was kindly loaned by Antonia Graham, and the one on page 128 was by HDG Studios and loaned by Anthony Bryant. The photograph on page 41 was lent by Aldus Archives with Syndication International, and the drawing on page 58 was borrowed from the Mary Evans Picture Library. The photograph on page 86 shows a card published by Prime Arts of Bath of the original pastel by Tony Hudson. The original of the photograph on page 51 was borrowed from the Peterborough Museum and Art Gallery under the Visual Arts hire scheme of Peterborough Arts Council. The photograph on page 63 was taken from a card produced by the Lincolnshire and Humberside Arts. The photograph on page 79 was styled by Susie Edwards around a window in her own home. All remaining photographs and locations are by the author.

INTRODUCTION

I love silk fabric, modern glass, cotton yarns, smooth wood and vibrant colours, clocks, hats, beads, old roses, new notebooks, heaps of pencils, soft leather and feathers, cutting and sticking, contrasting colours and kaleidoscopes, papier mâché, pastel shades and other people's homes. This profusion of passions is evident throughout the book in a variety of forms. Some inspire ideas, some are used as part of a design, and some feature as part of the room decoration seen in the photographed settings.

Although I cannot remember a time when I didn't sew or cut and stick, it was many years before all three techniques were combined on canvas. Once introduced to needlepoint I realized that the controlled grid system paradoxically frees the imagination to experiment with colour, form and texture. I enjoy the sewing of the yarn onto the canvas and share with fellow needleworkers the relaxing quality of the craft.

While not wishing to forgo the pleasure of needlepoint, neither do I wish to waste time. Time is the only real hurdle to creativity – while ideas may come from sources such as those shown in the book, the time to develop them has to be allocated and the degree of priority given to that is up to the individual.

This book does not offer to teach needlepoint; there are many excellent books available which teach stitches and how to use canvas. I would like to encourage an approach to the craft that shows a similar application to that which sportsmen give their hobby, and to describe methods that make best use of skills, equipment and precious time. There should also be an element of attempting something new. There is no right or wrong, only your own method – and remember,

A pretty 'basket of fruit' design has been worked on one of the cushions opposite (see project on page 35).

nobody is going to mark your work. You will always be your harshest critic, but I hope that some of the practical tips that are included with every project will help you reach your desired standard of finished needlepoint.

I wish there was a star system for the degree of difficulty, but even this could be misleading. I say this because I have learnt over years of producing kits that often it is the novice, someone who has never worked on canvas before, who sees the chart afresh and follows the lines without question and is thrilled with the result. On the other hand, others who are skilled and trained in all aspects of embroidery bring preconceptions to a chart that do not exist. There are few named stitches included here – the whole thing is more a matter of ideas, colour, texture, light and shade. A new enthusiast may find that

Testing new yarns (see page 16).

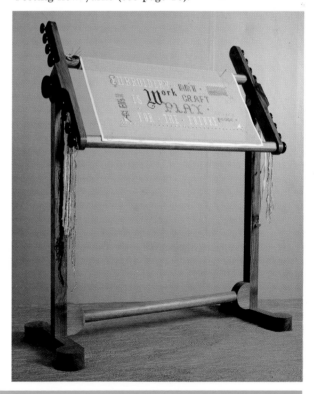

to plunge in at the deep end is easy; others may see the directions as so many hieroglyphics. To the latter I would say, be patient with the decoding. While every care has been taken to show close-up details of how each basic design was worked, the text may actually hold the solution to the problem.

Colour choices are extremely personal and, while I have included some bold combinations to illustrate that they do 'work' together, I really want to tempt you to try your own variations. I believe that tackling the question of where it is to go, before starting the project, reduces the chances of it being abandoned before completion. On the other hand, if the needlepoint is worked for a specific location it is too easy to choose colours that exactly match existing furnishings, and this tends to preclude innovative selections. Think more in terms of co-ordinating some of the shades. The sources of each project cover many decades and the colours chosen incorporate the shades that fit present interiors and hopefully endure frequent fashion changes.

I find architecture and construction interesting, but homes are more fascinating than houses, with the personalities of the owners evident at every turn. The individual choices of colour and memorabilia that some can arrange so artistically and effectively create an ambience for people to feel comfortable or 'at home'.

This book is intended to show the interested embroiderer how to develop basically simple ideas using personal flair. You will see how to build patterns and choose colours and how to produce work of a good finish with the details that make every article special and ready for display in its own particular place.

There are many uniquely crafted items throughout the book, as I enjoy craftsmanship in all its forms. The lovely part about combining other crafts with needlepoint is that it has been a pleasure to work with the people concerned who have unselfishly given their time. I would like needlepoint to be as skilfully worked as the other crafts shown here, and to encourage you to work with the same loving care.

EXPLANATIONS

GUIDE TO VOCABULARY

Books written in the English language travel to many continents where the technical vocabulary may not be the same.

I have generally used the word 'threads' to describe the canvas structure; 'sewing threads' describes dressmaking cotton to differentiate between this and all other fibres used for embroidery which are referred to as 'yarns'.

The measurements are metric, with imperial measurements in brackets. There are some inconsistencies in the conversions as I have sometimes used the nearest suitable practical measurement, so that, for example, half a metre equals half a yard, but when necessary I have been as accurate as possible.

To avoid references to alternative American vocabulary throughout the text, a few words are listed here:

stranded cotton – embroidery floss
cushion – pillow
pelmet – valance
tie-backs – curtain ties
wadding – batting

The 'wadding' referred to can be any suitable fabric to pad the work. There is a proprietary product of polyester available in various thicknesses, but any well-worn old fabric that can provide a soft underlay and rounded finish to your work is suitable. The thickness is not important as long as it is not too bulky and does not interefere with the shape or any calculated measurements.

I have used the term 'strong clear adhesive' throughout the book. Purists can still lace their work over card but technology now provides good-quality dyes, glues, protective sprays and cleaning fluids which all help to maintain the appearance of needlepoint. I have used a product called Uhu for many years and find it has a strong bond and shows no sign of discoloration even on the most delicate fabrics. I am frequently told of other glues, traditional and new, so leave it to you to use your favourite or accept advice from your specialist shop. Whichever you choose, do follow the instructions. Note that small tubes save accidents and waste, however tempting the economies of bulk buying.

A 'film of adhesive' means that a zig-zag poured from the tube is then spread evenly and very thinly with a flat edge. The surface is not impregnated with glue but there is sufficient to make a good bond with another surface that is similarly covered.

GUIDE TO THE PROJECTS

The background grids of the charts represent the interwoven thread of the canvas. The dark lines moving in different directions represent the yarn sewn over the canvas. This is sometimes over a single thread or a number of threads, straight, diagonal, twisted into a knot or woven. Colours are marked directly over the relevant stitch; any similar pattern not labelled should be repeated in the stated colours. The background tent stitches are often not completed, but the direction is indicated. If the chart is not able to explain itself, there are photographs, close-ups and explanations in the text to assist.

Diagrams

With each project there are diagrams of any detailed methods, cord edging or beading required, and if a cord is to be used for finishing, a diagram is given as a reminder. The precise instructions may be found elsewhere in the book.

Stitches

Tent stitch, continental stitch, diagonal tent stitch and basketweave (so named for its appearance at the back of the work) all describe a diagonal stitch over a single thread, taking the longest possible route. I do most of my work on the diagonal as I prefer the mesh of the stitches. Try to avoid half cross-stitches except when the design makes it necessary, as they alter the texture and wear, which is a false economy.

The stitches are not named as I think this intimidates those who are not 'in the know' and excludes them from sharing the fun. Those of you who are skilled with stitches can enjoy recognizing them, but beware if they appear a little unconventional. Stitches are not of prime importance. What they do is to add another ingredient to the permutation of direction, texture and light to give more pattern interest.

GUIDE TO EQUIPMENT

Frame and canvas

An even tension of stitches can only be achieved by working on canvas that is tautly mounted on a straight frame. This assists with the freehand designs that carry a yarn across the back past a number of threads. If the canvas is handled you destroy the dressing on each thread which gives it the firm structure. It is then necessary to strain the canvas back into a usable shape. Save yourself unpleasant tasks; when the canvas is removed

For details about the tools and accessories shown opposite, refer to the drawing, and list of materials on this and the next page.

from the frame, a light press on the back with a steam iron will smooth the fibres and 'block' the work ready for making up, but let it dry completely before handling.

A warning note here about temperature and humidity: try not to introduce your work to changes of temperature and humidity, either climatic or artificial. Avoid doing needlepoint on the beach or in the sauna if at all possible!

Tools and accessories

1 **Frames** These have recessed backs suitable for mounting finished pieces of work.
2 **Antique bobbin** Small quantities of commercial and antique lace can be stored this way.
3 **Shaker sewing box** Beautifully made and lined to hold and protect all sewing needs.
4 **Shaker pincushion**
5 **Spreader or trolley needle** The thick eyeless needle is mounted on a holder to slide over

13

the middle finger of the non-sewing hand. With the needle lying underneath, it can be placed close to the canvas and when multiple threads are laid over it, a slight movement back and forth will spread each thread so that they all lie flat and smooth. Invaluable for large areas of satin stitch with stranded cotton.

6 **Scissors** Those illustrated are old ones, but Germany still produces excellent needlework scissors. It is not size that is important, but the fineness of the points and the precise meeting of the two ends.

7 **Bronze leather** Here it is prepared and cut ready to use as a sewing thread.

8 **Wooden thimble** Decorative but useful for measuring beads.

9 **Beeswax** Only suitable for a firmly spun yarn that tends towards twisting and knotting. Useful for smoothing sewing thread when assembling a piece of work.

10 **Chatelaine** Based on the name for the set of tools carried on a chain by the mistress of a country house, the term has been adopted by embroiderers. These solid brass tools include a needleholder, a needle threader and a ripper blade to complete a 'sewing quartet' set with the heart-shaped beeswax. The ripper blade is most suitable for seams – use with caution on canvas.

11 **'Lo Ran' project card** This is part of the 'Filofax' of the embroiderer. The efficient, well-equipped student carries all yarns in a folder of cards similar to this. The project card has nine holes to loop yarns through and an area to record the shade numbers. There is a small magnet to hold some needles. The storage cards are larger and have ring holes punched ready for filing. All left-over threads can be returned to the file cards where they are protected, and by avoiding handling and friction during tangled storage, there is less wasted yarn.

12 **Stitch blade** It has a curved blade that is sharp to the tip and is ideal for isolating a tiny stitch even of a very fine yarn. The shape avoids any damage to the canvas.

13 **Stitch fixer** This tool has a fine angled hook at one end and a forked prong at the other. It can be used to adjust any uneven tension of stitches, poke short threads into place, and assist in weaving ribbons.

14 **Antique sewing-egg** This is a collectable rather than a functional item, though it does have an integral needleholder and a bobbin for two threads.

15 **'Butterfly' separator** This is a small piece of plastic with a short slit at the centre. Anything that prevents the handling of yarn is an advantage as manufacturers go to considerable trouble to provide yarns with a particular finish; handling only destroys that finish, particularly under warm conditions with moist hands. This tool allows one cut end of the yarn to be slid into it and, by separating the desired number of threads at the other, the 'butterfly' acts as a weight and spins as the threads are pulled gently apart.

SILK FABRIC YARN

Ribbon embroidery is well documented in needlework encyclopedias. Silk fabric can be used like yarn and applied in the same way. The fact that silk compacts into a very small space led me to use it as a yarn on canvas. At first I used different-coloured pieces of silk and the shades created with the light falling on the folds were quite satisfying, but the subtle shades of hand-dyed silk were introduced to me through Alison Bell's work. I was fortunate in being able to use her skills, but it is possible for anyone to produce their own silk fabric yarns.

The sample in the photograph on page 15 was dyed purely to emphasize and illustrate the yarn-making technique and to look pretty. Start with two colours and use well-diluted craft or domestic dyes to achieve a soft shade. A 50 cm (18 in.) length of inexpensive lining silk is most suitable and will give enough yarn for a first project. Dye opposite ends a different colour, letting the two merge towards the centre. The fabric can be left cramped and twisted in the dye bath to achieve an uneven absorption of colour. After it is dried and ironed, tear the fabric into 50 cm (18 in.) strips 1 cm ($\frac{1}{2}$ in.) wide. It is important to tear the fabric in order to keep straight lines with soft edges. The frayed sides

Dyed silk fabric for yarn

soon disappear among the folds when the strips are sewn through the canvas. Strips need to be 2 cm ($\frac{3}{4}$ in.) wide to work effectively on 14's canvas as for the 'Basket of Fruit' on page 35, but 1 cm ($\frac{1}{2}$ in.) yarn was used on 18's canvas for the mirror frame on page 122.

WORKING CONDITIONS

Hobbies often become passions that make us forget the passing of time. With needlepoint, that means hours of sitting in the same position. Do give your working method some thought.

Posture

I have a favourite chair which is comfortable to sit in and is the correct height. The right chair has to have a seat that supports under the thigh, with the legs at right-angles to the floor. Sit with your back supported and maintain the hollow at the small of the back with an extra cushion. My 'lumbar roll' is a small bolster, moderately firm, 10 cm (4 in.) in diameter. Perhaps the first project from this book of designs should be to adapt the bolster (see page 128). Sew with your arm supported at the elbow, resting one arm against the body, the other on the frame, flexing at the elbow to sew – a good reason for using a short yarn. Over-reaching with a long yarn causes

strain that will increase tension at the shoulders and neck.

Do get up and walk around at regular intervals with a few gentle, slow stretches if you can (see Bibliography, page 139).

Light

Work in good light. In the daytime the light should come across the work towards your working arm to avoid casting a shadow. With artificial light, a spotlight over the work, with background lighting as well, should be sufficient to be comfortable. Ensure that your eyes are healthy with regular check-ups and that your spectacles are suitable for the task.

It is essential to select colours in natural light, but avoid brilliant sunshine and snow-reflected light, as they have a bleaching effect on colour and the choice made in some conditions can be brighter than intended.

Winter is the time of year when there is more time to sew but paradoxically when the light is at its worst. I find that a halogen spotlight gives the natural light to continue colour selection, but there is a daylight bulb available from art shops which can be fitted into a regular light fitting and is extremely useful.

Try out new colours and patterns when you are feeling enthusiastic and use the hours of artificial light for repeating colours in background areas. Large borders are ideal to sew when you are feeling a little tired, as the rapid cover and the stitching rhythm of working on canvas is quite relaxing and a good antidote to solving the chart!

PREPARING A PROJECT

The sportsman's remark that 'the more I practise the luckier I get' could apply to embroiderers. Preparation and exercise are all part of the work. Be responsible for your project by solving as many of the questions as possible at the beginning so that you will not waste time when you consult your specialist shop.

Answer positively the simple questions: where is it to go, what is it for, do I want to finish it during a holiday or convalescence, do I want to give it away, will it be an antique of the future? Think in terms of cost, not just of materials but also that most precious cost — time. You have to really love the design, the work and the person for whom you are making the piece to invest perhaps 150 hours of your life on a single item.

I have given the dimensions of each finished piece of work on a specified canvas. If you wish to use a different size of canvas, this can be calculated before you go to purchase.

Use a measure marked with both centimetres and inches, because canvas is graded by the number of threads to the inch even where metric measurements have been adopted.

If the item measures 30 cm (12 in.) and is worked on a canvas 18 threads to the inch, the total number of threads covered is $12 \times 18 = 216$. If you want to work on a canvas with 14 threads to the inch, this thread count has to be divided by 14: $12 \times 18 = 216 \div 14 = 15.4$ in., which converts to 39 cm, which is the size the item will measure on the larger canvas.

Remember, if the canvas is changed the yarn required will also be different. Be practical when choosing a yarn — the thickness alone does not determine the strength. The type of fibre, the length of fibres, combined with the amount of spinning and number of ply, give varying strengths. The characteristics of different fibres is an interesting subject and well worth exploring through spinning and weaving techniques.

A yarn that is new to you should be tried and tested by working a sample. The sample started on the frame (see page 9) is my way of testing new yarns gathered on my travels. The piece is not going to suffer any wear, and total cover is not necessary, which enables me to use the yarns freely while assessing the friction and the covering ability during use. It is experience that judges the adjustments to be made, with a further test to prove it!

I wish I had a magic formula for calculating quantity of yarn required. It would save so much anguish and frustration. All needleworkers develop their own methods of working, and habits once formed are difficult to change. Generally, most students I see use a yarn that is too long by my standard. So how can one person calculate for another with so many variables? Only you know how you start or finish your work, or even how long a yarn you use. Add to this the working environment, with the cat, the dog, the vacuum cleaner and the side of the chair all secretly consuming threads. To illustrate just one of these problems, let us play with three skeins of 8 metres ($8\frac{4}{5}$ yards) in length.

Divide one skein into 24 lengths, one into 20 lengths and one into 16 lengths. If we assume that 10 cm (4 in.) was used each time for starting and finishing, we have a set of figures like this:

24×10 cm (4 in.) $= 240$ cm (96 in.)
20×10 cm (4 in.) $= 200$ cm (80 in.)
16×10 cm (4 in.) $= 160$ cm (64 in.)

The figures represent the wastage on *one* skein. Multiply that by the number of skeins used in a project and it is not surprising that sometimes we 'run out'.

In the dining room opposite, the Victorian theme is carried through to the photographs and hanging band.

Designers can only say how much was used in a particular design with their own method. Preparation for kits includes three or four different needleworkers giving their own estimates, and an average calculation is made from these estimates.

The items in this book are generally worked with short lengths, about 35 cm (14 in.), to maintain the quality of the yarn. However, if four or more threads are used for stitching, the yarn is used up more quickly, and double lengths are more suitable. The principle is the same: to limit the number of times that the needle and thread pass through the canvas.

To know the quantity before you start, it is imperative that you use your normal technique when working the sample. Work a 2.5 cm (1 in.) square with yarn cut to a specific length. Count the number of lengths used to calculate the total length required per square inch. Be generous with your calculation – remember the variables in your life!

If you have all this information at your fingertips, the knowledge builds confidence and will increase the enjoyment of putting your own project together. Do not equate this seriousness with dullness; it should all be fun – searching for materials, gathering it all together bit by bit, setting the canvas on the frame ready to go.

Each project described here has information in the form of standard headings, which are the answers to specific questions. Use the same headings at the start of your own project to help clear mind of a tangled web of questions.

Transfer this information to a postcard for your shopping trip.

Item	What is it?
Use	Where is it to go?
Dimensions	How big is it?
Canvas: size	How many threads to the inch?
: quantity	What are the dimensions, plus 10 cm (2 in.) border?
Yarns: type	Brand? Colour?
: quantity	How much of each?
Needles: size	Which is suitable?
: other	Beading or stitching?
Other materials	Ribbons, beads, fabric?

FINISHING TOUCHES

Have you noticed how often people lift up the skirts on a doll the moment they are presented with it? With an embroidered object they always turn it over. This is not the occasion to discuss why people do it, but it illustrates that all work must be finished to withstand close inspection. Each project includes guidelines about making it up, but a few general notes might help.

It is important to think of the item as a whole project and to gather together the fabrics and trimmings along with the yarns, before you start work. Yarns can be adjusted to match a backing fabric far more easily than the other way round. Choose fabrics that fold easily, as they need to stay in place as you work with them; avoid the slippery satins and jerseys. Try to use the best-quality materials you can. Avoid wasting time by good planning, and store left-over yarns carefully. Make a small item with any remaining yarns from a project, as they are already co-ordinated and you have learnt how they look together. An additional skein of one shade may be sufficient to complete the design (see the 'Flame' panel on page 72).

Whenever it is necessary to cut the canvas close to the stitches, make sure that a film of glue seals the area before cutting. Then the canvas can be used like any other fabric.

Use borders and the cord edging stitches to surround a design and give a finished edge.

When the design runs to the edge, perhaps it could run over to the back with a few embroidery stitches and beads applied to the backing fabric.

The cords and tassels can be made as extravagantly as you wish. They can be incorporated into the design as well as used as an embellishment.

There are ageing processes that can be used on textiles like those employed by theatre-set designers, but washing and dyeing are effective and simple. A commercial trimming that looks a little too new in tone can be dyed with a very weak solution of 'old gold' dye (but do *not* dye the needlepoint). The washing is part of the process that damages the trimming slightly and adds to the 'old' look. Tea and coffee can also be used, but with a very absorbent item the amount of coffee dye needed tends to leave an aroma as well! The curtain fabric and the fringing on page 64 were dyed in this way. Always dye trimmings before attaching them to allow for shrinkage. A fabric treated in this way will probably shrink and can create interesting textures, with mixed fibres reacting differently.

Articles like boxes and containers that are covered with needlepoint cannot be dry-cleaned, and it is difficult to advocate a treatment, but such items can be sprayed with a fabric protector. A regular gentle vacuuming to take away the damaging dirt particles is the best care.

CORD EDGING AND CORD-MAKING

When a design is surrounded by a cord edging, a symbol similar to Figure 1 is shown with the chart. Two- and three-colour cords are described here, but any number of colours can be used.

The cord edging is worked by using the thicker yarn. Starting at a corner, work over one thread diagonally but four threads along, then back under two threads and over four again, in the

Fig 1 cord edging

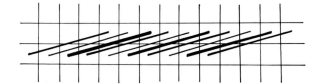

form of an elongated tent stitch. The second yarn is then worked in the alternate vacant holes, laying it over the previous yarn rather than pulling it through too tight. Figure 1 shows the yarns as straight lines but in reality they curve round each other, which is why I call it a cord edging.

Start at a corner using the hole outside the thread that is to be the base for the cord. Cover the four threads to set the pattern, then return back to the starting hole and over two threads before continuing in a regular pattern. The second yarn needs to go over one thread and three threads at the start.

Work as described above until the last stitch enters the hole past the thread that is the base for the cord. Take the next two or three stitches that are necessary to complete the row, into the same hole, and turn the corner by starting at the same point as at the beginning.

Different effects are achieved by mixing the yarns. A base yarn that is bulky can have a fine yarn laid over it, or equal yarns can fit side by side. Do not change the order of working at a later stage as this will affect the appearance.

When you come to make up the item you will see the neat finish and appreciate why it is used on so many of the designs.

Cord-making

When a cord is part of the original design, a symbol as seen in Figure 2 is shown with the chart. The following describes the method used.

The thickness of the yarn has to be decided on first. To do this, take the yarn you intend to use and fold it a few times, twisting it tightly between your hands. Adjust the number of folds until it makes the thickness of cord that is needed. Count the number of threads used and

cut that number for your project. They need to be three times the length of the required cord and tightly twisted together until they start to kink. To achieve this, make certain all the threads lie together under the same tension, and tie the ends together in a knot. Place one knot over a hook and slip a pencil just inside the other knot, holding it in place with your other hand. Wind the pencil which will in turn twist the cord – the tighter the twist, the better the quality of the cord. When the kinks appear under the hand next to the pencil, it is ready for the next stage which is to fold the twisted cord in half. An assistant is very useful at this stage as one hand needs to be placed at the fold to keep it temporarily apart, and one hand has to take the pencil to the hook. A third hand is therefore required because the distance between two hands is not always sufficient for the length of cord!

The assistant holds the two ends parallel, so that the cord making can start at the folded end. Pinch the fold together and move 5 cm (2 in.) along, pinch the twists together, and the cord will form under your hand. Continue the pinching with alternate hands, maintaining a tension until the end or it will spin out of control and knot. Smooth the new cord between your finger and thumb, accentuating the twists at the same time.

Different colours can be blended together or two colours can be looped through each other at the middle with the same colour ends knotted together. When twisted and folded the resulting cord is two-toned as applied to the curtain tie-back on page 64.

The large tassel hanging near the curtain seen in the same picture has a fine cord as part of its design and a thick cord attached made from the same fine yarns.

The trimming on the seat cushion on page 118 was made with Appletons crewel wool. Because there were an uneven number of threads in each section, the dark cord appears to wind itself around the multicoloured threads, but it was achieved by the same cord-making method.

When you are practising cord-making, use short lengths, but enough for the successful pieces to be attached to a tassel and a key as seen opposite and in the cupboard door on page 17.

Fig 2 cord making

One tassel is decorated with beads and another has four rows of stem stitch worked in each row of loops, which emphasizes the spiral pattern and makes a very firm head, while buttonhole stitches decorate the base of the cord.

TASSELS AND TASSEL-MAKING

There is a renewed interest in tassels and trimmings in the world of soft furnishings. The appreciation of craftsmanship combined with an interest in the past reaches beyond nostalgia to a genuine concern about our heritage.

Pages 138 and 139 show a variety of tassels displayed on some beautifully embroidered fabrics at 'The Green Room' in Suffolk. If you are not fortunate enough to see antique textiles for sale, there are stately homes the world over with examples at the windows. Museums also house collections, but I find this less satisfactory as the very tactile nature of textiles is lost behind glass –

although, of course, even those on show in stately homes should never be touched. It is the old, worn textures that appeal in antique textiles, and the intricate detail of handmade fringing and tassels is fascinating. Even with modern production techniques, much of the work is still done by hand and the modern colour combinations are just as stunning as those from the past.

There are samples of tassels throughout this book. The degree of detail is entirely in the hand of the designer, but be warned – they can be as compulsive as needlepoint!

Pat White has been good enough to explain her tassel-making technique in diagrams. A fine example of her work can be seen on this page and *in situ* on page 17. This tassel is worked in a Lucy Coltman dyed silk with gold thread decoration.

Tassel-making

It is easier to practise with thick yarns using a contrasting colour for covering the head of the tassel. This can be your sample for future reference and the easier it is to see the working method the better.

The type of the yarn is not important, as synthetic fibres can be as exciting as silk, but the profusion of yarns is the key to a successful tassel. The head needs to be covered with a smooth-finished yarn, one that is tightly spun.

Consider the tassel's proportions before you begin. Allow extra length for the amount taken up in the head and for levelling off.

Method (*see diagrams overleaf*)

1 Wind the yarn round a piece of card or a similar object to obtain the required size and bulk. Err on the side of too much if in doubt. Cut off the yarn at the level of the tassel bottom.
2 Cut about 1 metre (1 yard) of yarn and tie a knot away from one end, leaving a tail the length of the tassel. Using a tapestry needle thread the yarn through the top of the tassel loops.
3 Take the needle through the yarn under the knot.

Fig 3

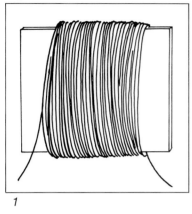

1

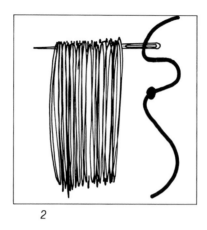

2

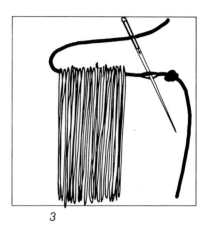

3

4

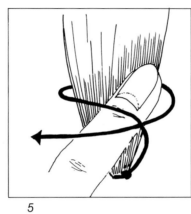

5

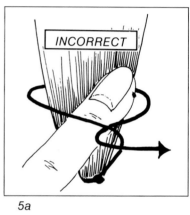

INCORRECT

5a

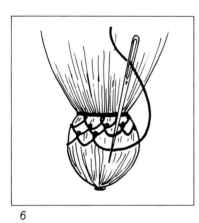

6

7

8

9

4 Pull the yarn tight and secure with a small stitch. The tail of the yarn left beyond the knot will smooth down and become part of the tassel if it is the same colour. If it is a contrasting colour, trim the end.

5 Holding the tassel with the head towards you, take the threaded length of yarn down to the depth you want the tassel head to be, wrap round fairly tightly, holding it with your thumb and taking the yarn through the loop. It will seem natural for you to pull the yarn against the loop at this stage, but if you try this you will see that it distorts the head of your tassel, so pull it in the same direction as you are winding and wrap round once more. Secure the winding by taking the needle through the wrapping yarns.

6 With the tassel in the same position, begin stitching using a detached buttonhole stitch round and round. The first row is secured to the wrapped yarns and the subsequent rows follow the previous loops. The size and tension is as you wish, but there has to be some adjustment to shape the head by loosening each row towards the centre and tightening as you continue the curve. If you find that while you are working the head is not firm enough, take a little yarn and wind it tightly into a ball and push it into the centre of the head.

If you run out of a yarn, mark the place with a pin in the last loop and use the same method as for finishing described in stage 8. To resume stitching knot a piece of yarn and bring it through the centre of the tassel, coming out at the loop marked with the pin.

7 As you approach the top of your tassel, stop so that the cord can be attached. Ideally the cord is looped so that the two ends can be joined. These are laid side by side and securely stitched in place with a matching sewing thread. Trim the ends carefully.

8 Continue with the buttonhole stitch. When you see that you are working towards the end, begin to reduce the number of stitches by working every other loop. This decrease is quick and shapes the rounded top. Push the cord down slightly and hold in a central position with the closing stitches.

9 Cut the loops and trim neatly, checking the proportions

The tassel is now ready for decorating, which can be done as creatively as you wish.

Overleaf: detail of woodgrain bolster (see page 128)

PROJECTS

VICTORIAN PINCUSHION

Black papier maché items with a mother-of-pearl inlay have fascinated me since I first saw some furniture of my grandparents. The menu holder seen here with the lily-of-the-valley motif is seen again on the clock on page 17, and is typical of the Victorian period. The pattern on the clock face surround was adapted to suit the canvas and repeated to fit different items: the pincushion, the fingerplate and the cushion. I chose to decorate the door of the dining-room to link with the clock. The pincushion is shown on a small plate stand, but can be used to display a collection of hatpins or brooches.

The Victorian theme is continued with the application of beads on the pincushion. Figure 4a (overleaf) gives a detailed drawing. This theme is repeated by any chart where beads are used as part of the design.

My experiences in America frequently confirmed the belief that we are peoples divided by a common language; for instance, 'fingerplates' or 'doorplates' are unheard of, but 'switchplates' are readily available. The plate for the door covers the area above the door handle that is frequently held by the fingers when using the door. The 'switchplate' surrounds the light switch to protect the wall or wallpaper from fingermarks. Whichever shape is available to you, both are transparent plastic shapes with a recess in the back to hold paper, fabric or embroidery.

Beading

When using beads as applied decoration, the canvas is covered with embroidery first and the beads that are added as ornament can be of any shape or size. On the other hand, when the beadwork is part of the needlework and applied directly to the canvas, the size has to be taken into consideration. Although the beads are held by a diagonal stitch on the crossed threads as seen in Figure 4a, the size to suit each canvas is the size of the hole between the threads. If they are too big, they are difficult to sew and they manoeuvre each other out of line. A sewing thread for applying beads will endure the friction of wear better than a single strand of embroidery cotton. Use a matching colour which needs to be a shade duller or darker so that it appears as a shadow on the finished work. Secure the thread to start with by breaking all the rules; with a knot at one end, pierce the canvas thread from below and pass round the diagonal threads before coming up in the hole below your first bead. The fine bead needle will not damage the canvas.

Work in the same way as tent stitch for a single row or with diagonal tent stitch for filling areas. Fasten off securely. It does help to work with light coming from behind the canvas so that you can see the holes clearly to bring the needle through, as the bead conceals your view.

The beads themselves are awkward to handle, but there are various methods of keeping them under control, like spreading them out on a cork mat or a strip of sticky tape fixed to the frame with beads adhered to it. My favourite time-saving method is a small double-sided sticky pad which will lift between twenty and thirty beads and can be fixed to the top of your non-sewing forefinger. This method allows the angle of the bead to be manipulated so that the needle can lift off one at a time as work is in progress.

Chart: See page 28
Dimensions: 12 × 12 cm (4$\frac{3}{4}$ × 4$\frac{3}{4}$ in.)
Canvas: 18's mono canvas de luxe 20 × 20 cm (8 × 8 in.)

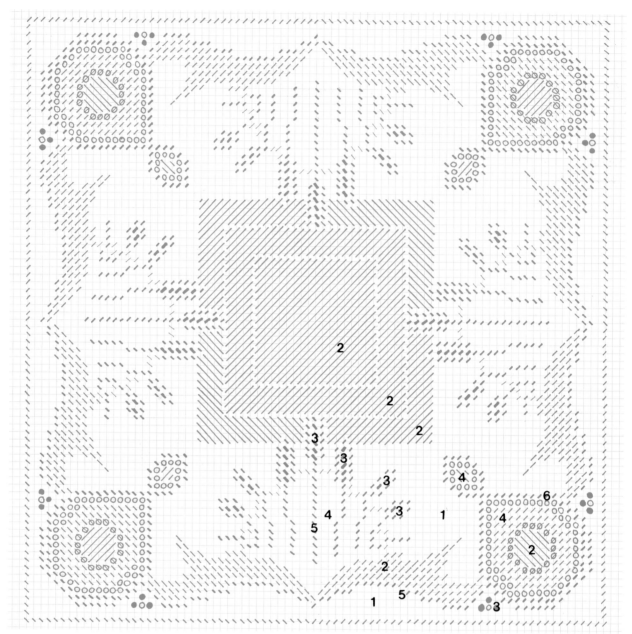

Pincushion chart

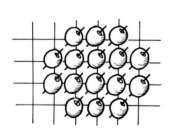

4a   beads sewn onto canvas

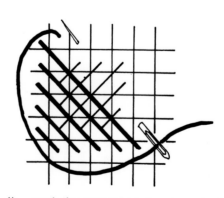

4b   work the central square to a double thickness.

Colour code

1	Anchor 403
2	DMC Ecru
3	DMC 309
4	Anchor 212
5	DMC 3047
6	Anchor 924

4c French knot

Yarns: Stranded cotton, used as it comes from the skein. One skein of each unless stated otherwise
DMC Ecru × 2 309 3047
Anchor 403 × 3
924 212
Needles: 20's tapestry, beading needle
Extras: 1 thimbleful of pearl or creamy beads
3 thimblefuls of glass gold beads
Backing fabric 14 × 14 cm ($5\frac{1}{2}$ × $5\frac{1}{2}$ in.)
Suitable filling, e.g. bran
Sewing needle and thread to match
Notes: It is easier to apply the beads after working a few of the nearby stitches (see beading notes on page 27).

Method

1 Measure and mark out the shape on your canvas as a guide.
2 The central square can be worked to a double thickness to give a very smooth, silky appearance (see Figure 4b). The circles surrounded by pearls are double thickness, achieved by simply repeating the charted stitch.
3 The outline is set by colour number 2. The part to be worked next is up to you. The background stitches have not been completed so that the pattern can be seen more clearly, but watch the changing direction of the stitches.

Adaptation: This design is suitable for a switchplate. Change the central square and work it in tent stitch to the shape of the commercial plate. The beads must be substituted by french knots as on the fingerplate (see Figure 4c).

Making up

1 Trim the canvas with a 2 cm ($\frac{3}{4}$ in.) seam allowance.
2 Place the embroidery face down on the backing fabric.
3 Machine or back stitch in the holes with the outside yarn, sewing round all four corners but leaving a gap of 5 cm (2 in.) on one side.
4 Machine round again, checking that the stitches are as close to the sewing as possible.
5 Trim the fabric to the size of the canvas and cut across the corners.
6 Fold back the seam allowance at the gap and press to give a firm crease.
7 Turn it inside out.
8 Cover the embroidery with a piece of fabric sealed at the top with masking tape.
9 Pack with bran (available from health food stores), about 125 g (5 oz). Pack it tightly, using a knitting needle to get it firmly in the corners. The floury dust only appears at this stage, which is why the embroidery must be protected.
10 The creased seam allowance gives the lines to be joined by ladder stitch. This in-and-out running stitch allows the two edges to be pulled together invisibly. Fasten off ends securely. Use a long, fine needle so as not to distort the fabric or canvas and to achieve the desired neat finish.
11 Shape the pincushion with your hands, tapping it to remove surplus dust. Remove the protecting fabric.
12 A piece of silk rubbed over your work will 'polish' it.

Door Fingerplate

Chart: on this page

Dimensions: 25×5.5 cm ($9\frac{3}{4} \times 2\frac{1}{8}$ in.)

Canvas: 18's mono de luxe, 35×15 cm (14×6 in.)

Yarns: One skein of each unless stated otherwise

Stranded cotton

DMC Ecru × 2 309 3047

Anchor 403 × 4

924 212

DMC divisible thread Gold

Needles: 20's tapestry

Extras: Transparent fingerplate with recessed back

Clear adhesive

Notes: This chart fits a specific commercially available plate, so please check measurements and adjust before you start. Position eyelets for the fixing screws.

Colour code		
1 Anchor 403	**5**	DMC 3047
2 DMC Ecru	**6**	Anchor 924
3 DMC 309	**7**	DMC Gold
4 Anchor 212		

←This stitch represents the centre of the pattern. Do not repeat when reversing the chart.

With two-sided patterns it is ideal to have a hole as the centre point (as we have between top and bottom), but when making an item to fit a specific shape there is no choice. In this design the central

5a French knot

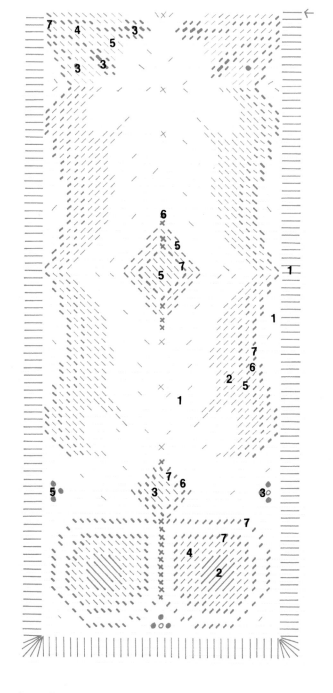

Door fingerplate chart

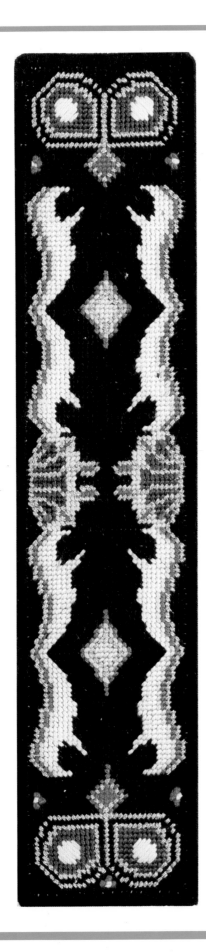

canvas thread has to be covered and it is used as the change-over point for the stitch direction. This makes it into a cross stitch, which is indicated on the chart. Note the direction of the background stitches, all worked in colour number 1.

The gold thread is used with three thicknesses of the yarn, which loops rather easily, but the free hand at the back of the work can keep the loops untangled and make progress easier. The twisted threads catch the light and are an ideal substitute for the beads.

Method

The chart is half the total design. The arrow at the top is the centre stitch and when the chart is turned upside down to complete the design, the central side stitches are not repeated.

1 Measure and mark the shape in the middle of the canvas as a guide. Mark the halfway point.
2 Start at the arrow on the halfway point and work the chart to the bottom.
3 If you turn your frame round, the pattern can be repeated as it is printed; note the centre stitch.
4 Start with colour number 7 which will set the pattern.

Making up

The eyelets are placed for the fixing screws. Prise them open a little to allow the screw through. It is necessary to keep the embroidery as slim as possible to fit into the recess of the plate, so there is no extra backing.

1 Trim the embroidery with a 2 cm ($\frac{3}{4}$ in). border of canvas.
2 Spread a film of clear adhesive on the canvas border and to the same distance around the embroidery.
3 Trim the corners and fold in the turnings, making sure that no canvas is visible.
4 Leave under a board and weight until glue is set. As the work is to be covered, the texture will be largely lost.
5 Press into the recess of the plate and it is ready for placing on the door.

HANGING BAND

A search for a way to arrange a group of Daguerreotypes led to the hanging band, which can be seen on the left of the fireplace in the picture on page 17. An early photographic process produced portraits on glass plates surrounded by decoratively etched gold metal which are set inside a leather-covered frame. The leather has a small patterned border printed with gold, and it was a selection of these that gave the designs for the band.

The needlepoint provides a firm support for the small frames, as it is interlined and backed. Choose colours to suit the situation and adapt the size to suit your collection of pictures, but the project size described is suitable for commercially available photograph frames such as the one that can be seen on the right of the fireplace in the picture on page 17.

The hanging band is composed of border patterns set side by side. Each of them can be used in another situation – see the border pattern in the picture on page 134 and the cushion in the picture on page 110.

Chart: See opposite
Dimensions: 4 × 41 cm (1½ × 16¼ in.)
Canvas: 18's mono de luxe 50 × 10.5 cm (19½ × 4 in.)
Yarns: One skein of each unless stated otherwise
Anchor stranded cotton 842 852 858 896 895 683
DMC divisible thread Gold
DMC coton à broder 2221 × 2
Note carefully the number of strands used throughout
Needles: 20's and 22's tapestry
Extras: Iron-on adhesive tape 4 × 50 cm (1½ × 18 in.)
Backing fabric or ribbon 4 × 50 cm (1½ × 18 in.)

Frames of a suitable size × 3
Strong needle
Sewing needle and matching thread

Notes: The straight stitches numbers 4 and 5 are worked with four strands. The background number 7 is worked in three strands. The gold thread is worked in three strands. Number 4 at the side is best worked with four strands because the hole is filled with the soft cotton.

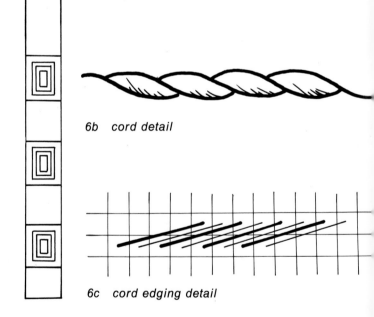

6a   hanging band detail

6b   cord detail

6c   cord edging detail

Colour code			
1	DMC coton à broder 2221	**5**	Anchor 858
2	DMC Gold thread	**6**	Anchor 896
3	Anchor 842	**7**	Anchor 895
4	Anchor 852	**8**	Anchor 683

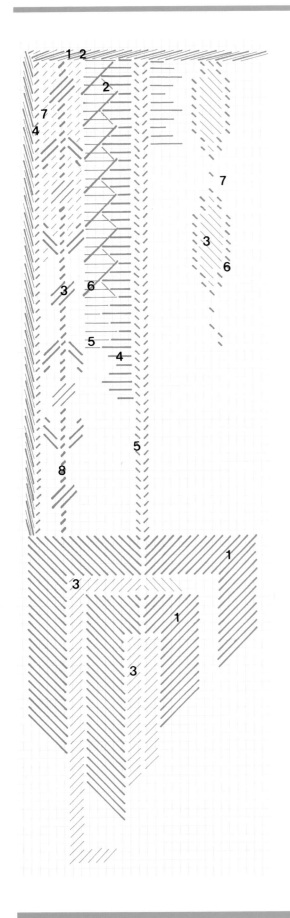

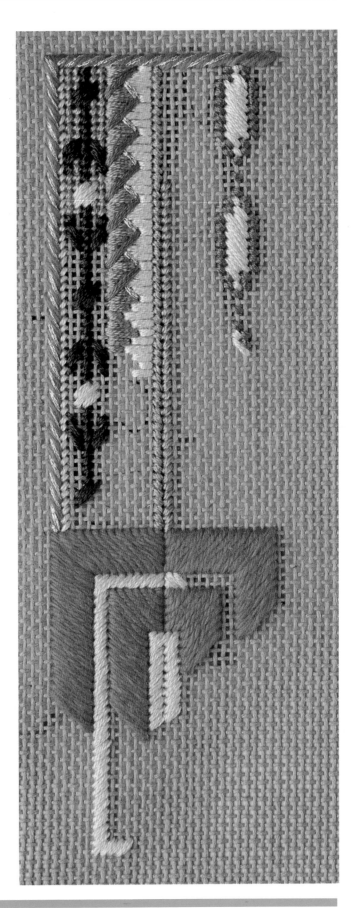

Method

1 Start 5 cm (2 in.) from the top of the canvas at the centre.

2 Work the tent stitch middle.

3 Work the straight stitch zig-zags numbers 4 and 5.

4 With the gold thread, work over one side of the point covering two threads and go back to work over the other side of the point carrying the gold thread over four threads of the canvas, (see the photograph on page 33).

5 Work the pattern shapes of the other borders before the background stitches, the direction of which is indicated on the chart.

6 The border patterns can be continued but the area to be covered by the frames is worked in wide bands.

7 The pattern continues 5 cm (2 in.) between the rectangles and 4 cm ($\frac{1}{2}$ in.) at the bottom, as shown in Figure 6a.

8 The cord edging is worked in two colours. See page 19 for details of working.

Making up

1 Cut embroidery from frame with a 2 cm ($\frac{3}{4}$ in.) border of canvas.

2 Cut iron-on adhesive tape to fit the length.

3 Press the canvas edges to the back, leaving the cord edging right on the edge so that it appears to have been applied to the outside, not to the front.

4 Cut away excess canvas at the corners.

5 Apply the frame ties by using six strands of cotton and a strong needle. Align the frames and mark the point of attachment. Using six strands of cotton and a strong needle, pierce through the layers, work a small securing stitch and come to the front two threads away. Leave enough thread to tie the frames in place with a bow after completing the next stage.

6 Make a cord with remaining yarns (see page 20).

7 Fix cord by glueing 2.5 cm (1 in.) of the ends to the back, near to the sides.

8 Turn in the seam allowance at the top and bottom of the fabric or ribbon backing. Hand stitch to the front edges; this can be done quite invisibly. Make certain that extra stitches secure the cords at the top edge.

9 Tie the frames into place.

The commercial frames available may be free-standing. The stand can be removed to give a bar by which they can be attached.

Adaptation: The borders can be separated out and used as described above. Alternatively the whole pattern can be used as a tie-back or pelmet border with or without the rectangular areas.

'BASKET OF FRUIT' CUSHION

The resurgence of stencilling as a form of decoration gives the most modest artists a chance to express themselves. A pattern emerges through someone else's design, or the more ambitious can cut their own stencils; either way the placing of the decoration demonstrates individual creativity. Simple motifs on boxes or elaborate friezes around rooms are well-documented ideas, but a stencil can also be applied to canvas, either as an outline or coloured in with fabric pens.

The first tassel shape on the pelmet on page 79 was drawn using a stencil that was used to decorate part of my workroom. With canvas embroidery there is no need to re-stencil the image as the stitches used in the first image can be copied, unless the pattern is to change angles, like a group of tassels tied together.

There is a unique texture to stencilling and the softness of one thin colour laid over another was the instigator of the 'Basket of Fruit' design. The gentle shades of the coton à broder and the texture of the silk fabric yarn are an integral part of the design. The finished cushion can be seen on page 8.

A simple stencil design

Charts: See pages 36 and 37

Dimensions: 'Basket of Fruit' panel 21.5 × 21.5 cm (8½ × 8½ in.)
Border 9 cm (3½ in.)
Total 39 × 39 cm (15½ × 15½ in.)

Canvas 14's mono de luxe 50 × 50 cm (20 × 20 in.)

Yarns Silk fabric yarn – see page 14. One skein or hank of each colour unless stated otherwise

DMC coton à broder 2373 2778 2950 2407 × 2	If not using silk fabric, add the following colours: 2758 2495
DMC Medici wool 421 505	101 328 125 503
Anchor stranded cotton 259 880 1209 860 956 859 843	292 260

Needles: 18's tapestry

Extras: Backing fabric 46 × 46 cm (18 × 18 in.)
Cushion pad 40 × 40 cm (16 × 16 in.)
Sewing needle and matching thread

Notes: This all looks more complicated than it really is. Figure 7b shows the stitch guide for a 'rose'. The yarn forms a curve around the starting french knot and the size of each flower can be developed as you wish.

This design has an element of free design that is well worth attempting. The basket, which covers half the area, is charted. The arrangement of fruit is also charted, but can be rearranged.

The list on page 39 describes the yarns and colours for each part of the chart. Consult this carefully, as the chart is numbered with alternative yarns.

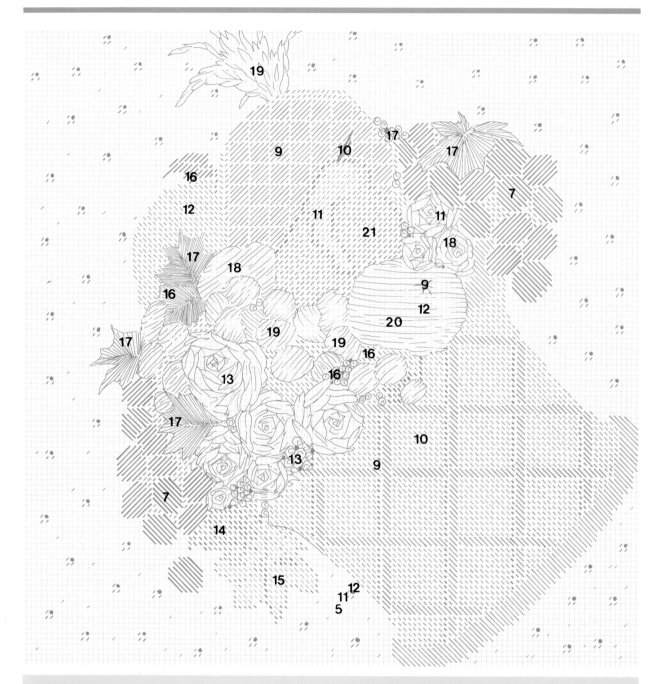

Colour code

1	Peach silk fabric	**9**	DMC coton à broder 2950
	4 threads of 101 DMC Medici wool	**10**	DMC coton à broder 2407
2	Grey silk fabric	**11**	Anchor 259
	4 threads of 125 DMC Medici wool	**12**	Anchor 880
3	Yellow silk fabric	**13**	Anchor shaded 1209
	4 threads of 328 DMC Medici wool	**14**	Anchor 860
4	Grey/green silk fabric	**15**	Anchor 956
	4 threads of 503 DMC Medici wool	**16**	Anchor 859
5	DMC Medici wool 421	**17**	Anchor 843
6	DMC Medici wool 505	**18**	Anchor 292
7	DMC coton à broder 2373	**19**	DMC coton à broder 2495
8	DMC coton à broder 2778	**20**	DMC coton à broder 2758
		21	Anchor 260

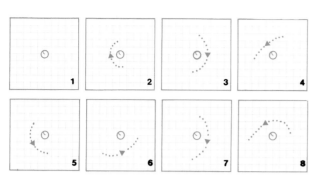

 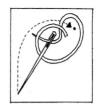

7a   French knot

7b   stitch guide for a rose

◀ 'Basket of Fruit' chart
Border chart (below)

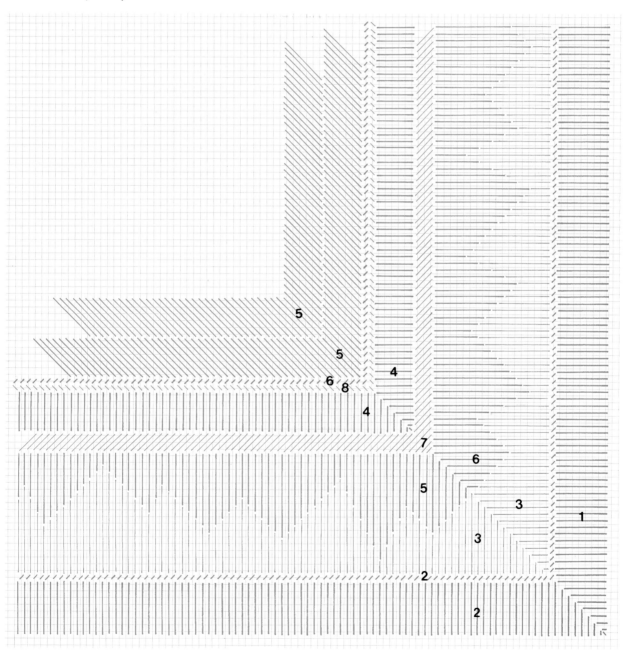

Silk yarn is used on this design. The finished
cushion can be seen on page 8.

Detail of the border

Method

1 Measure and mark the outline of the cushion.

2 Run a sewing thread diagonally in each direction.

3 Draw another line 9 cm ($3\frac{1}{2}$ in.) inside the previous one, in each direction from the diagonal thread. The area inside this line is charted on page 36.

4 Start with the basket by counting from the corner and begin with colour number 10 at ↑.

5 Once the base is complete, the exact line for the border is established, and this can be worked at any stage. The diagonal thread indicates the point to turn the corner.

6 Finish the basket and then place the fruit. A sketched arrangement will help. Note that the pineapple leaves encroach onto the border. Consult the close-up photograph (page 38) which is shown with part of the border.

7 The background is worked in three strands of Medici wool with three small stitches in stranded cotton and a contrasting french knot. Not only is this for the embroiderer's benefit to vary the background, but it offers a little extra for those who are interested in the work, as an item is more intriguing for not giving away all its design at one glance.

8 Complete the borders.

Making up

Make up the cushion as described on page 73.

Adaptation: This is only really suitable as a cushion when worked with silk fabric yarn. However, if it is worked in wool and cotton it can take more wear and would look very attractive inset as a diamond-shaped panel for a bedhead, either singly or as a pair.

	Charted colours	Substitute yarn colours
Basket	9	
	10	
Background	5	
	11	
	12	
Apple	Shaded silk fabric peach to mauve; 16 stalk	9, 12, 13, 20; use nine strands of Anchor
Pear	Shaded silk fabric green to yellow; 10 stalk	11, 21; blend nine strands together
Leaves	16	
Knots	17	
Filling stitches		
Roses – mauve	Shaded silk fabric	13; use twelve strands
green	Shaded silk fabric	11, 18; use together as twelve strands
Grapes –	Shaded silk fabric	19
green	7	
'black'	Shaded silk fabric;	20 with 12 in six strands worked over the top
Orange	9 stalk	
Pineapple	9	
	Green silk fabric	19
Lemon	Yellow silk fabric	18
Vine leaf	15	
	14	

CONTAINER

The Newport pottery jug painted by Clarice Cliff illustrates the strong lines of her designs and the colours that are associated with the Art Deco period. The name of Clarice Cliff is synonymous with this period, and her present popularity is reflected in the prices of work attributed to her. The cream bowl here shows another aspect of her designs, with the representation of crocuses again in strong colours. There are several books on designs of the period that offer considerable detail (see the Bibliography on page 140), but there may be a piece of pottery in the home of an older relative that could suggest interesting new patterns or colours.

Taking inspiration from the Art Deco period, the original idea for this design was a container for table napkins, either paper or fabric, but definitely nothing heavy as the card frame is hand stitched together. For illustration purposes the candles allowed all the embroidery to be seen, but the size and shape showed them to be tailormade for the curved container and proved to be a very satisfactory alternative. A detail of the container can be seen on pages 44 and 45.

Charts: See pages 42 and 43
Dimensions: Back 12 × 21.5 cm (5 × 8½ in.)
    Front 30 × 11 cm (12 × 4½ in.)
    Total 25.5 × 21.5 cm (10 × 8½ in.)
Canvas: 18's mono de luxe 30 × 60 cm
Yarns: 1 skein of each unless stated otherwise
    DMC Medici black wool × 2
    Stranded cotton
    Anchor 245 261 306 212 305 297 324
    122 × 2 403 × 3 386 × 3
    DMC 550
Needles: 20's tapestry, beading needle
Extras: Commercially produced cord 50 cm (18 in.)
    Fabric 30 × 100 cm (12 × 36 in.)

Narrow (3 mm) double-sided satin ribbon 10 cm (4 in.)
Acid-free card for backs and base
Flexible stiffening (self-adhesive stiffening is ideal)
Strong clear adhesive
Sewing needle and matching thread
Notes: Read the advice on beading on page 27, and fabric-joining on pages 113 and 114. Any yarns carried across the back must be worked over to secure them at an even tension, because the work is to be curved and the tension on the outside will be greater than that on the inside, which would allow any loose yarns to adapt and so alter the smooth appearance of the surface.

Newport pottery jug painted by Clarice Cliff

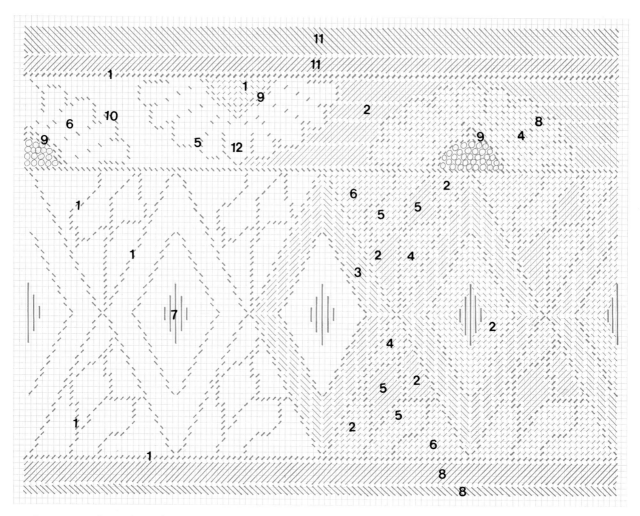

Art Deco container chart: front

Colour code

1	DMC Medici wool Black
2	Anchor 386
3	Anchor 305
4	Anchor 306
5	Anchor 212
6	Anchor 122
7	Anchor 403
8	Anchor 324
9	Anchor 245
10	DMC 550
11	Anchor 297
12	Anchor 261

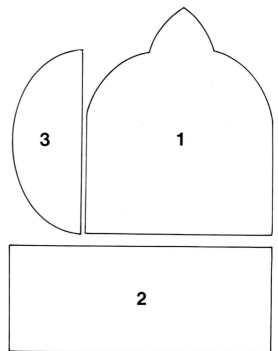

Fig 8a   template

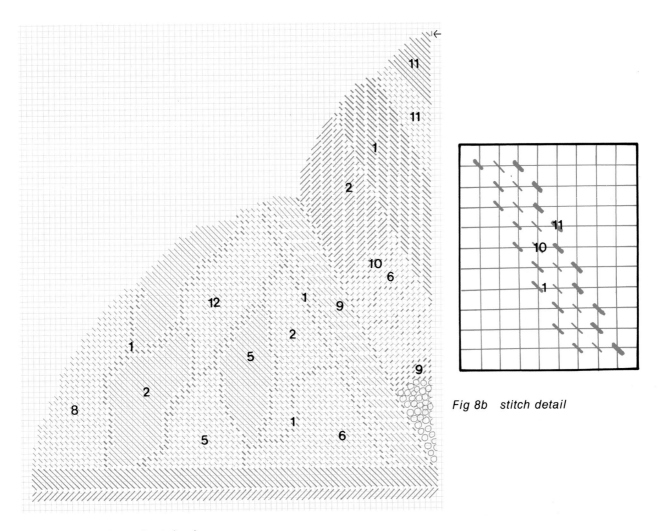

Fig 8b   stitch detail

Art Deco container chart: back

Method

There is a template shape in Figure 8a. This is a guide to the total shape which is required for fabric and card, but it is better to measure your work and adjust the template when you have finished. This template is *not* the layout for the needlepoint.

1 Working directly on the canvas, measure and mark the front piece (Chart opposite), on the canvas at top right, leaving a border of 5 cm (2 in.).

2 The back piece has half the chart only (above). The ↓ marks the central stitch and is not to be repeated when the chart is reversed and repeated. The piece is positioned at the left side –

remember that the top is to be embroidered and the rest is to provide a base for the fabric lining. The remaining piece of canvas is available for the adapted design for a small pocket.

3 Work the colour number 1 areas first, and number 7. To avoid the hair of the wool from discolouring the pale thread next to it, the needle should pass *over* the yarn at the back and not through it. Complete all other parts as you wish, watching for the changes in stitch direction.

4 The flowers are best outlined first as shown on the chart, before completing the background.

5 There is a detail in Figure 8b to show the rows of different colours on the back pattern.

6 The beading is crowded. It is worked as shown in Figure 8c.

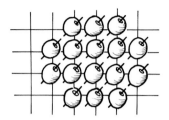

Fig 8c bead detail

Making up

1 Pieces of fabric and card must be cut for the embroidery, so a paper template is essential. Trim the paper to fit the shapes exactly and use as patterns for the card, adding a seam allowance for the fabric.

2 A piece of fabric 33 × 14 cm (13 × $5\frac{1}{2}$ in.) is applied to the edge of the back embroidery and stitched to the canvas while still on the frame. This forms the inside lining.

3 Now the pieces are to be cut from the frame, each with a border of 1.5 cm ($\frac{3}{4}$ in.), but if you plan to work that little piece of spare canvas it is best to do so while it is still attached to the frame.

4 Cut two pieces of card in the shape of (1) and two pieces of (3) in Figure 8a.

5 Cover one piece of (1) with the embroidered canvas, folding over the edges neatly, and hold in place on the back of the card with some clear adhesive. NB Only the hidden edges on the reverse side have adhesive.

6 Cover the other piece (1) with fabric in the

Pages 44 and 45 a detail of the container

same way and stick the two pieces together, sealing in the fabric turnings. Place right side down on a soft rug or carpet, cover with a board and weight until needed.

7 Cover the two pieces of (3) with fabric and repeat the above process.

8 Cut the stiffener to shape. Check with the template that it fits the inside of the embroidery when curved.

9 Stick the stiffener in place and fold over the canvas so that none of it is visible from the front. Use clear adhesive to fix the edges in place.

10 Hand stitch the lining to this piece, remembering to keep it taut as it is to curve inside. For the same reason, this piece should not be pressed.

11 Fix a loop to the centre of the back section using a strong needle. Insert the ribbon from the back to the front, take across 1 cm ($\frac{1}{2}$ in.) before returning to tie at the back. Cover those yarns that are the same colour as the ribbon, and the loop will be invisible from the front.

12 Join each side of the embroidered front to the fabric sides of the back, using small sewing stitches. The base is fitted inside the semi-circle and hand stitched into place so that it is not visible from the front. On the one that I made there was a slight discrepancy in the joining, but I decided this was an advantage, as the tiny gaps in the corners would allow any crumbs or dust to fall through instead of collecting there. Always be ready to adapt!

13 Finish by fixing the cord round the join of the back pieces. Trail a line of adhesive into the gap and press the cord into place.

How to fix cord: Pinch the end of the cord and cut across close to the fingers. Immediately apply clear adhesive to seal the ends, but leave for a moment before rolling the ends between the fingers, thereby maintaining the twist. Fix the cord in place but do not cut until the length is almost completely fixed. When 2.5 cm (1 in.) from the last fixing point, an accurate measurement of the length can be made and the cutting and sealing process repeated.

Adaptation: Use part of the front pattern to make a small pocket (see page 48). Colours have also been given in the Chart on page 49 for the container to be made in pastel shades.

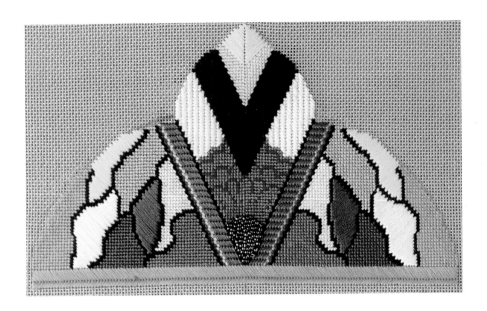

Above: the container back

Below: the container front

SMALL POCKET

This envelope-shaped container can hang by the bed to keep rings or a watch safe overnight.

Chart: See page 42

Dimensions: Embroidery 13 7.5 cm ($5\frac{1}{8}$ × 3 in.)

Completed pocket 8 × 8.5 cm ($3\frac{1}{8}$ × $3\frac{1}{4}$ in.)

Canvas: 18's mono de luxe 13 x 18 cm (5 × 7 in.)

Yarns: Anchor stranded cotton, one skein of each

875 386 892 893 276 942

Needles: 20's and 22's tapestry, beading needle

Extras: Narrow (3 mm) double-sided satin ribbon 50 cm (18 in.)

10 small beads, 5 sequins

Fine fabric 8 × 20 cm ($3\frac{1}{4}$ × 8 in.) for lining and backing

Sewing needle and matching thread

Notes: Number 7 is the same colour as number 1.

Method

1 Measure and mark out the rectangular area on the canvas as a guide.

2 Work a diamond pattern starting at the left-hand side and then turn the canvas over.

3 Leave a space the size of the diamond worked by counting threads and then work the next diamond as well as the surrounding stitches to complete the shape as shown opposite, right.

Making up

1 Turn the canvas back again. Before taking it from the frame, cut a piece of fabric to line the pocket and stitch to the side of the diamond. If you start by cutting the fabric down the centre to fit the point and then stitch up each side, the excess fabric can be cut away from underneath afterwards.

2 Trim the canvas to three threads around the embroidery and the equivalent on the sloping sides.

3 Match the fabric to the same size and tack to the sides with overstitches.

4 Starting in the centre of the V, snip to allow turnings and secure the fabric firmly to the canvas before continuing up each side, joining the fabric to the embroidery edge.

5 Cover the back of the pocket by turning a hem and tent stitching it to the embroidery edge. The stitches will pass through the lining fabric and will help to secure the fold.

6 Take the fabric to the top and allow a sufficient turning to fold over. Join the fabric to the embroidery at the front of the work.

7 Trim the sides and tack with overstitches.

8 Cut a small loop of ribbon and fix at the top point, with a bead at the front and a bead and sequin at the back. The bead acts as an anchor for the sequin, which is a pretty cover for the fixing stitches.

9 The ribbon is the right width to cover three canvas threads and, as there is little room for error, a small needle is advisable for the couching stitches. When the pocket is folded into shape with all the embroidered surface to the front, the ribbon is sewn into place with three strands of cotton in a toning colour. Start at the base to secure with an overstitch, and then the fabric and canvas is sandwiched between the ribbon with a diagonal overstitch evenly spaced to give an equal line on each side. The needle returns in the sixth hole along.

10 By pulling firmly, the edges of the ribbon will come together at the outer edges to conceal the layers underneath.

11 Fold ribbons prettily and secure back and front with sequins and beads.

Colour code
1 Anchor 875
2 Anchor 386
3 Anchor 892
4 Anchor 893
5 Anchor 276
6 Anchor 942
7 Anchor 875

If using this colour scheme for the container, the following colours will complete the pastel theme:
8 Anchor 386
9 Anchor 213
10 Anchor 876
11 Anchor 894
12 Anchor 02

MIRROR FRAME

The work of art that prompted this design was available on a three-month hire scheme from a local authority. Do enquire into the possibility of borrowing works of art in your area. It is more like a fostering scheme as you must care for the piece without getting too attached to it. 'Evening' was very difficult to give back!

The canvas is an obvious basis for geometric design and I intended to include a formal, repetitive pattern in this book when I saw Philip Brown's woven paper (right). The subtle shading of graphite and the softness of the pale gold achieved by staining with coffee is impossible to reproduce in textile work. In any case, copying is not the aim; the idea and its impact are the inspiration. I avoided total repetition by varying the yarns and lightening the colours to pale shades in one corner.

Chart: See page 52
Dimensions: 40 × 40 cm (16 × 16 in.)
  Border 10 cm (4 in.)
Canvas: 18's mono de luxe 50 × 50 cm (20 × 20 in.)
Yarns: Danish flower thread HF32 × 2, HF19 × 1
  Medici wool 8327 × 5
  Stranded cotton
  Anchor 400 × 5 399 × 5 874 × 4
  DMC 3024 × 6 746 × 6 Ecru × 7 3046 × 2
  Use three strands of flower thread, two strands of wool, and the stranded cotton as it comes from the skein.
Needles: 20's and 22's tapestry
Extras: Materials for making the mirror (see page 54)
Notes: It is not necessary to repeat exact patterns over a large area; the textile industry can do this better. The creativity of the needleworker allows change to take place at any point and this design is a good example of

needlepoint achieving uniqueness where fabric weaving cannot. I have used two shades of cream which are difficult to separate in artificial light but do add to the subtlety.

Method

1 Measure and mark out the outside frame area on the canvas; this defines the amount to be worked and appears less daunting than a bare canvas.
2 Start with colour number 1 in the bottom left-hand corner and work a back stitch diagonally

'Evening' by Philip Brown

51

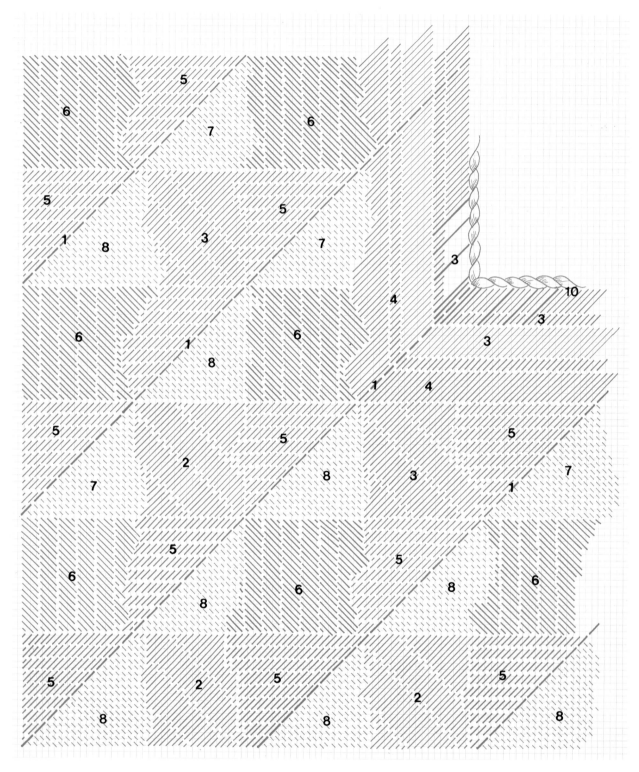

Mirror frame chart

over two threads. Following the chart to the inside edge of the frame.

3 With a spare thread, follow this line accurately to the opposite corner. This will help to line up the diagonal lines and to check counting.

4 There are 36 threads between each diagonal row and 18 threads in each lateral band. A straight line can be drawn along the line of holes at this point if you wish.

A detail of the mirror frame which clearly shows the direction the stitches are worked.

5 It is only the vertical lines that are wiggly ('torn') and you can draw your own or follow the chart on page 52.

6 Once the corner has been worked as illustrated, a section of the pattern can be repeated, remembering that to have the proper effect the designs meet at each corner.

7 Start the inside border as soon as you can, as this marks the 200 cm² (80 sq. in.) that holds the mirror and does not have to be stitched. Note how some of the colours are carried through to the next colour at the corner just as a point of interest.

Adaptation: If an array of colour is used over the whole area it takes on a patchwork appearance to make a pretty cushion for a bedroom. Could it be the answer for all your spare yarns? I worked a spectacle case, seen opposite and on the desk on page 56. The changing directions of the stitches help to keep the work square, but it is always advisable to keep the work on the frame until you are ready for making up.

Making up

This method applies to all sizes but when the card is not strong enough to support the weight of the mirror glass, plywood should be substituted.

Materials for a frame

NB Use an acid-free card to avoid damage to textiles.

Backing piece

Surround, made of sufficient layers to equal the thickness of the glass plus adhesive pads

Front, cut a little smaller than the finished needlepoint to allow for the thickness of canvas and embroidery

Piece of wadding to fit

Mirror glass, cut 5 cm (2 in.) larger than the frame space

Double-sided adhesive pads

Backing fabric and lining

Two pieces of narrow polyester ribbon

Velvet ribbon or petersham ribbon

Strong clear adhesive

Small curved needle and sewing thread

Careful measurements must be taken to ensure that the front card fits within your work and that the backing card is fractionally larger, as the fabric covering is not as bulky as the needlepoint.

1 Cover the back with lining underneath the backing fabric that tones with the needlepoint.

2 Make two holes an equal distance from the top and proportionately from the sides to allow balanced hanging. Using two pieces of coloured ribbon, to give added decoration and strength, thread through the holes with all the ends tied together at the back. Glue down the ribbons looped inside the back.

3 Fix the mirror glass to the inside of the back with double-sided adhesive pads.

4 Glue together as many layers of the surround as are necessary to allow the front to lie flat.

5 Glue a layer of polyester wadding over the front and trim to fit.

6 Place a little clear adhesive at the inner and outer corners at the junction of canvas and stitches and leave to harden and seal.

7 Cover the padded frame with the needlepoint, working with it like a fabric. Cut into the inner corners and across the outside corners. Fold the canvas round the frame, making sure that the needlepoint reaches right to the edges. Glue into place evenly.

8 Weight the piece by placing under a board face down on a carpet or rug to absorb the texture of the work. This assures good adhesion and presses the piece to give a good finish.

9 Glue front to back and replace under the weighted board.

10 Make a cord for the inside edging using sufficient strands to conceal the reflected image of the back of the canvas. Run a line of clear adhesive at the junction of the front to the glass, pushing the cord gently into the gap to fix into place. If you use the folded end of the cord to overlap the cut end at the bottom left-hand corner, the join is virtually invisible.

11 The outer edge can be covered with velvet ribbon or petersham ribbon, as both are sufficiently textured to conceal the irregularities. A curved needle is useful to apply the ribbon with small stitches at the front and back. Leave a little ribbon before stitching so that at the end the scissors can cut through the overlapping ribbons to give an exact join.

SPECTACLE CASE

The chart for the spectacle case (see page 57) is only a guide to work from, and Figure 9a gives a colour chart for the spectacle case featured here. It was worked on 18's mono canvas in stranded cotton in the following colours: DMC 453 and Anchor 875, 895, 894, 892 and 216.

Making up

A spectacle case is a most pleasing size to work but I know that many needleworkers are disappointed with their needlepoint when it is made into a case. There were many failures before a solution was found to give a finish that matched the quality of the embroidery.

The underlying answer to the spectacle case problem lies in the cutting of the fabric. As well as this, it must be understood that canvas should never be turned inside out unless it is subsequently to be fully padded as with a pincushion or cushion. To do so breaks down the structure of the canvas irrevocably.

One method was devised to keep the needlepoint flat with a fabric lining and then a padded backing was made the same size and the two pieces joined together. Even this had some problems – I found that the canvas was easily led astray by the fabric, and after a period of handling and changes in temperature the whole case was distorted. My aunt came to the rescue with her dressmaking skills; she marked the fabric pieces by pulling out the warp and weft threads at the required measurements and then cut outside this line for the seam allowances, so ensuring straight sides. Using the fabric 'square' and joining it to canvas which is also 'square' prevents any chance of it moving askew.

While this method works very well, it is extremely time-consuming, so be careful before offering to make a dozen or so!

Small pieces of needlepoint can be made up into pretty pockets or cases.

1 Measure the sides of the embroidery.
2 Cut three pieces of fabric the same size by the method described. Remember to include a seam allowance.
3 Machine or back stitch one piece of fabric to the top edge of the embroidery and fold over on the join.
4 Turn all seam allowances in and ladder stitch the remaining three sides together. Press.
5 With the second piece of fabric, cut some wadding a little smaller than the marked area and hold in place with two rows of stitching about 2.5 cm (1 in.) apart.
6 Take the third piece of fabric and with the right sides together, stitch to the padded fabric. Machine or hand stitch round the three sides, matching the pulled lines exactly.
7 Trim the corners and turn inside out before hand stitching the open edges together.
8 Note that the top edges of the front and back are turned seams and the handsewn seams are to the base. Place front to back with the stitched lining to the inside.

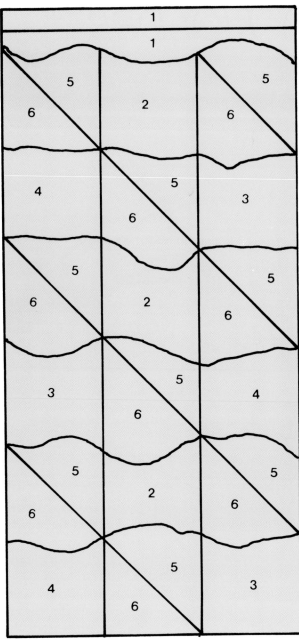

Fig 9a   *colour guide*

Spectacle case chart

Colour code			
1	Anchor 216	**4**	Anchor 895
2	Anchor 875	**5**	Anchor 894
3	DMC 453	**6**	Anchor 892

9 Using a toning yarn, secure the top edge with a few overstitches before continuing with a herringbone stitch that works with a figure-of-eight movement about 1 cm ($\frac{3}{8}$ in.) apart on either side. When you need to join a yarn, a knot through all layers from the inside is the most secure and will not be seen. Fasten off this end to match the start.

This method proves to be strong as well as allowing the case to pack flat or expand with the spectacles inside.

Opposite: spectacle case and stationery holder.

STATIONERY HOLDER

I am sure that calligraphy could be a source of design but for me the fluidity of its technique would be lost in the geometric structure of needlepoint. The fine vellums and interesting papers are far removed from the embroidered finish. It is fascinating to see the colours used in illuminated manuscripts and the intricate forms of modern calligraphy, but it was the quills of the scribe that prompted an interest in feathers, and so this design developed.

The variety of colour makes it suitable for any situation in the home, but the rigid containers lend themselves to a study, where they have a practical purpose.

The pure silk yarns used result in very special items that are always decorative, for example the stationery holder on the desk on page 56, and the box on page 61.

Chart: See page 60
Dimensions: 12 × 22 cm (4¾ × 8⅝ in.)
Canvas: 14's mono de luxe 22 × 30 cm (9 × 12 in.)
Yarns: There is sufficient to make both feather items excluding the background shades
Lucy Coltman tapestry silks, one skein of each unless stated otherwise
1002 1036 1027 1068 1046 1064 1070
1067 × 3
Needles: 18's tapestry
Extras: For making up
Acid-free card, two pieces 12 × 21.5 cm (4⅝ × 8½ in.), two pieces 18 × 21.5 cm (7 × 8½ in.)
Interlining, soft cotton fabric 30 × 60 cm (12 × 24 in.)
Backing fabric – silk dupion is most suitable – 30 × 75 cm (12 × 30 in.)
Block of wood 4 × 1.5 × 21.5 cm (1¾ × ½ × 8½ in.)
Felt for base
12 small brass nails and hammer
Strong clear adhesive

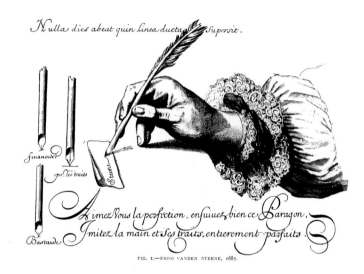

FIG. I.—FROM VANDEN STEENE, 1687.

It was the quill of the scribe that prompted the feather design seen here.

Notes: The silk tapestry yarn is lovely to work with but care has to be taken that the sewing movement does not change the texture. Adjust the turn of the needle accordingly, particularly with the straight stitches as they hardly cover the canvas. I felt this was a design advantage as there was some shadow between the threads which increased the feather effect and the surface was not to undergo any wear.

Using the silk thread requires the best-quality canvas so that the polished threads will not snag the fibres. This is definitely a design where each colour should have a separate needle, as the pattern is worked freehand.

Method

1 Measure and mark out the area on the canvas.
2 Work the diagonal stitch border to the line. The cord edging (see 6 opposite) is worked on the

thread outside the measured mark; this does not have to be completed at this stage. Once the border is started, the layout of the feather can be decided. The chart is accurately recorded if you prefer to count threads.

3 Work the main vein in colour number 6 and then the straight stitches beside it in colour number 1.

4 The numbers are placed over areas of colour so do not worry about the exact stitch marking. Consult the photograph below for guidance and use the colours in the style charted.

5 The background is dotted with a single stitch in colour number 7, which is marked on the chart. The stitches are randomly placed and counting is not important. The remaining background tent stitches are not marked but they follow the same direction. Use shorter yarns for the background to maintain the quality of the finish.

6 The cord edging is worked with three colours. Figure 10a shows a detail of the method. The main colour number 7 is worked first, leaving alternate holes for the other colours. There is no advantage in multiple needles as this interrupts the rhythm and subsequent neatness.

Making up

1 Cut the embroidery from the canvas with a 2 cm ($\frac{3}{4}$ in.) border.

2 One small piece of card has to be trimmed to fit inside the embroidered area to allow the canvas to fold completely over to the back, leaving the cord edging at the sides.

3 Spread a film of clear adhesive on the back of the embroidery and canvas, then cover the card as described above.

4 Cover the other three pieces of card with only the folded edges stuck to the back. The interlining is cut slightly smaller so that the fabric covers the edges on the back.

5 Sandpaper the edges of the block of wood and cover with fabric, folding the excess to the long sides where it will be concealed, and sticking the edges underneath.

6 Cover the base with felt or leather trimmed to fit exactly. Secure the edges firmly.

7 Stand the base on a flat surface and stick the fabric side of the small card to one side. Use six small nails to secure it in place, making sure the bottom edge is level with the base.

8 Repeat with a larger piece of covered card on the other side of the base.

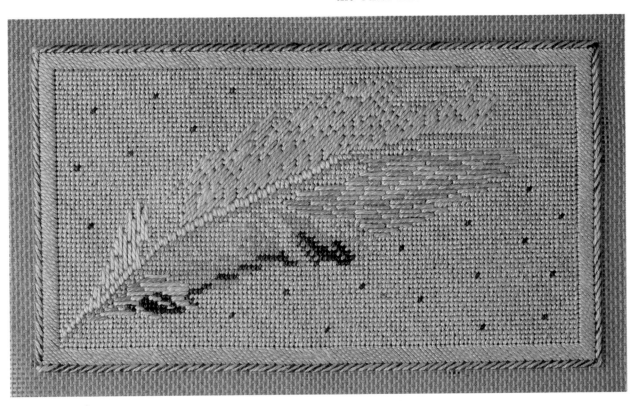

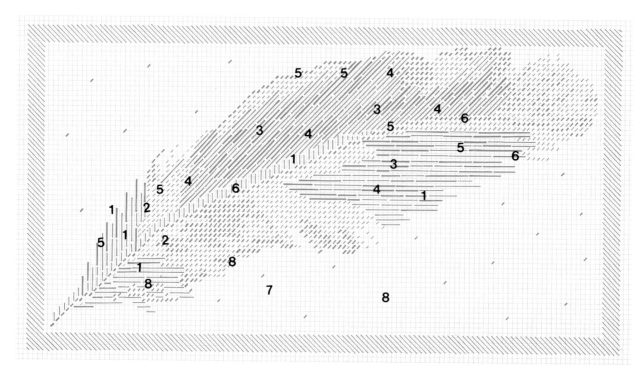

Feather panel chart

9 Stick the embroidered front to the matching card and make sure the adhesive is on both surfaces and right to the edges.

10 To press the two cards together, use magazines to pack the space between and place the holder on each side for an hour.

11 If you think the joins need covering, follow the instructions for finishing the container on page 46.

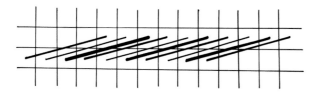

Fig 10a   cord edging

Adaptation: The covered surface can make a book cover or box lid.

Opposite. The feather design is worked on a dark grey background and the needlepoint is used to decorate a plain fabric-covered box. A tassel in matching colours completes the design.

BOX LID

The feather panel worked for the stationery holder has a pale background which gives the feather a soft outline. Working the pattern again on an 18's canvas, a dark surround defines the shape. The design is reduced in size but the surrounding area is increased to fit the box. This particular box was proportioned to fit the cards for a Victorian stereoscope. Decide on the purpose and size of your box, noting that the feather measures 16.5 cm (6½ in.)

Charts: Page 60 and below
Dimensions: 20 × 12 cm (7⅞ × 4¾ in.)
Canvas: 18's mono de luxe
Yarns: Lucy Coltman tapestry silk, one skein of each unless stated otherwise
   1002 1036 1027 1068 1046 1064 1070
   Continuous single colour 70 × 3
Needles: 20's tapestry
Notes: Follow the chart on page 60 for the feather pattern. There is a front border detailed below where the wider rows are randomly worked in three colours. The dominant colour matches the background and is worked first, leaving spaces for the next colours. Work this area last as you can assess the colours that are available, using as many as you wish.

Method

1 Measure and mark the area of the panel.
2 Work around the line with a single row of tent stitches in colour number 7 as the border.
3 Mark the size of the feather and work as described for the stationery holder. The silk tapestry yarn fits closely on the 18's canvas but is still easy to use.
4 I chose to work the background in four strands of continuous silk with a diagonal tent stitch worked in the opposite direction from the rest. Starting in the top left corner and working in diagonal rows, the hand-dyed yarn developed very subtle shading.

Making up

This panel was applied to a hand-sewn box that was made for me. A piece of petersham ribbon was attached to the inside base at the back, long enough for the cards to sit in place, but the tassel-decorated end can be pulled to lift them up for easy removal.

Jane Lemon has written an excellent book about embroidered boxes (see Bibliography).

Chart showing feather box detail

Colour code
Lucy Coltman tapestry silks
1 1002
2 1036
3 1027
4 1068
5 1046
6 1064
7 70
8 1070

LARGE CURTAIN TIE-BACK

Museums and galleries provide beautiful objects for our gaze, and opportunities to examine our own ideas by analysing and criticizing what we see. They are a training ground for looking and seeing with discernment, which is important if you are looking for ideas to use in your needlepoint. There are usually counters where reproductions of the exhibits are sold, and this is how I found the picture of the urn. I had missed seeing it on display but was attracted by the colours on the card. It certainly is an exciting piece of art and craft to create with papier mâché a shape that is 1 metre (3 feet) high. The decoration suggested to me the desert and Egyptian origins, with luxury and embellishment necessary for any soft furnishing. The kind of extravagant detail that is best worked on a single item to attract attention, combined with the dominant border theme, led to the single curtain tie-back with cords and tassels seen on page 64.

Charts: See pages 66 and 67

Dimensions: The diamonds at each end are 10 cm (4 in.) across
 Total length 49 × 10 cm (19½ × 4 in.)

Canvas: 18's mono de luxe 60 × 18 cm (24 × 8 in.)

Yarns: DMC Medici wool Black × 2, used in 3 strands
 DMC coton à broder 2407
 Zwikky silk floss 2129, used as it comes from the skein
 Anchor stranded cotton, one skein of each unless stated otherwise
 368 × 3 361 × 3 372 × 3 400 399 187
 DMC 3047 × 4 Ecru 504 × 2
 For the cord: Anchor 368 DMC 3047

Needles: 18's, 20's and 22's tapestry

Extras: 13 tassels
 Backing fabric 30 × 122 cm (12 × 48 in.)
 Wadding 50 × 10 cm (19½ × 4 in.)

Papier mâché urn by Julie Arkell.

Iron-on Vilene 50 × 10 cm (19½ × 4 in.)
Sewing needle and matching thread

Notes: The tassels can be handmade or cut from a length of manufactured trimming. Cut the thread that attaches the tassel to the braid and slide off the head, leaving a small loop ready for the needle.

There are a variety of yarns used in this project which adds to its interest. Coton à broder is a soft spun cotton that will either twist or unwind as you work depending on the motion during sewing. Adjust the yarn accordingly as you work to maintain an even texture. Too long a thread will be destroyed

by too much friction so take care to change your needle to suit the yarn, and at the same time keep to a size that minimizes the damage to the canvas.

Method

1 Measure and mark the area on the canvas as a guide.

2 The photograph on this page shows close-up details and the method of working pieces of pattern before the background.

3 Start one of the diamonds and work the bottom zig-zags to find the distance accurately before starting the other diamond. It is easier to count 'points' than so many single threads.

4 Work the large areas of straight stitches, keeping the threads as flat as possible.

5 The cord is applied when all other stitches are complete.

6 To make the cord, each of the skeins is divided in half, joined together at the centre and twisted following the instructions on page 20.

7 To attach the cord have two needles ready threaded with colour number 1. Bring the needle through at the border edge in line with the peak of colour number 3, one at the top and one at the bottom. With a small straight stitch over the row of tent stitches, hold the twisted loop in place. (Run each needle parallel to secure the next loop along each border edge.) The cord-making method provides a natural looping – just make sure there is a uniformity in the direction of each turn. The cord ends can be pulled through to the back and secured with a few small stitches. Knot the end of the remaining cord the moment it is cut as this will be needed later as a trimming.

NB Decide which way you want the curtain to be held back.

Making up

1 Leave the work on the frame.

2 Cut a template the shape of the needlepoint and to fit just inside the embroidered area.

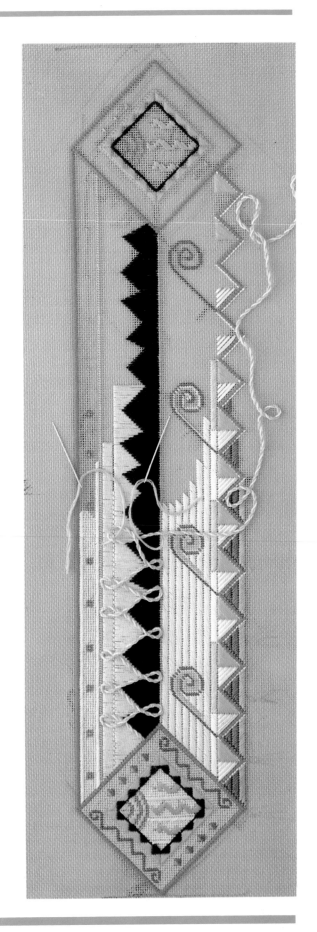

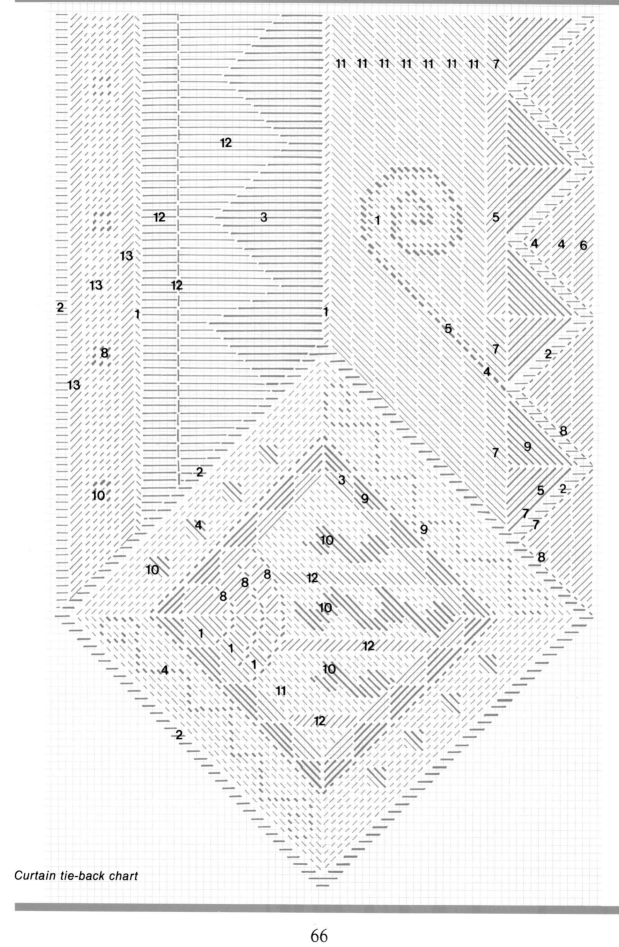

Curtain tie-back chart

Colour code

1 Anchor 368
2 108 wool
3 DMC Medici wool Black
4 Anchor 400
5 Anchor 372
6 Anchor 399
7 DMC Ecru
8 Anchor 187
9 DMC coton à broder 2407
10 Zwikky silk floss 2129
11 DMC 3047
12 DMC 504
13 Anchor 361

Fig 11a   cord detail

3 Cut a piece of fabric 56 × 15 cm (22 × 6 in.) and sew to the outside edge of the diamond at the middle of the curtain tie-back; see page 113 for advice on attaching fabric. The cotton chintz used was firm enough to cut and fold neatly under for sewing with a toning yarn.

4 Remove the needlepoint from the frame and trim away canvas to leave a seam allowance of 1.5 cm ($\frac{3}{4}$ in.)

5 Cut a piece of Vilene the size of the template and iron onto the fabric and the canvas diamond.

6 Cut a piece of wadding the size of the template. A thin film of clear adhesive will hold it in place on the back of the needlepoint. Make sure that some adhesive is on the point of the canvas to secure the stitches and to allow the excess canvas to be cut away.

7 Press the canvas seam allowance right back and follow the line through to press the fabric turnings over the stiffening.

8 Lay the completed front of the tie-back onto the wrong side of the remaining piece of fabric, press the turned seam allowance under and cut away excess fabric at the corners. Matching the shape exactly, hand stitch the edges together all the way round.

9 Sew the tassels in place at the edge of the points. Secure each end of the sewing thread in the canvas, with the attaching stitches loose enough to allow the tassel to swing.

Adaptation: This would make a very exciting mirror frame or, by reversing the borders, a wide band suitable for a bell-pull or wall hanging.

I chose to work part of the border and used it round a wastepaper bin (see page 70, where it is seen by the table). When working designs for yourself, shapes like the curly patterns can be different each time: use the chart as a guide, not as a doctrine.

WASTEPAPER BIN BORDER

This design idea is not fully charted.

Chart: See below
Dimensions: 5 cm (2 in.) deep

The border was worked 66 cm (26 in.) long to fit round the top of a plastic bin bought as a plant container. The bin has straight sides, so covering it was quite simple.

A row of alternate tent stitches as illustrated in Figure 12a was added as a finishing edge.

The following yarns were used: Orchidee pure new wool in shades 2221, 2223, 2216, 2217 and 2143; Eva Rosenstand and Clara Weaver's stranded cotton in shades 199, 140, 196, 197, and 145 for the background × 6 skeins.

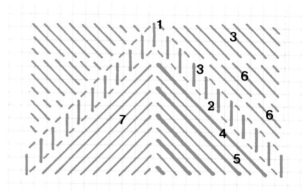

Chart showing stitch detail.

Colour code

1 Orchidee wool 2223
2 ER/CW 199
3 ER/CW 140
4 ER/CW 145
5 ER/CW 196
6 ER/CW 197
7 Orchidee wool 2143
8 Orchidee wool 2221
9 Orchidee wool 2216
10 Orchidee wool 2217

ER/CW = Eva Rosenstand and Clara Weaver's stranded cotton

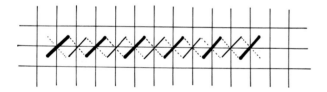

Fig 12a   stitch detail

Wastepaper bin border chart

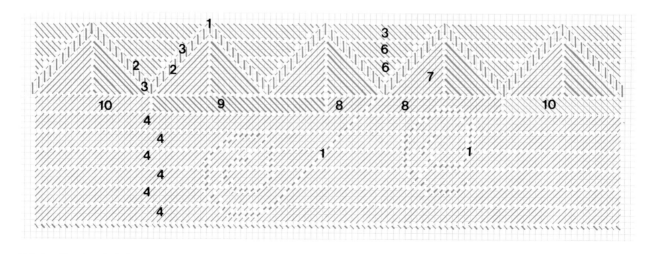

When measuring round your container, do so with a strip of folded canvas and carefully mark the join. (A tape measure would distort the length needed.)

Making up

1 Cut the embroidery from the canvas with a 1.5 cm ($\frac{3}{4}$ in.) seam allowance. Fold the top under and hold with a little clear adhesive at one end. Glue the border to the top of the bin and fix the folded end firmly over the flat seam allowance.
2 Cover the remainder of the bin with a piece of leather. Cut notches in the bottom edge and glue to the underneath. Cover the base with a circle to conceal the ends. I matched the yarns to the piece of leather, which is easy to cut and glue as it has no fraying edges, but ultra-suede or felt would be suitable substitutes.

If a pattern is adapted, the ends will not match. To do that, the measurements must be taken first and the pattern proportioned to fit the size.

CUSHION INSET

Charts: See page 72 and border chart on page 73

Dimensions: 12 × 12 cm (4¾ × 4¾ in.)
Border 1.5 cm ⅝ in.)

Canvas: 18's single de luxe, 20 × 20 cm (8 × 8 in.)

Yarns: Stranded cotton, one skein of each unless stated otherwise
Anchor 893 × 2 213 892 847 778
DMC 746 × 2 739

Needles: 20's tapestry

Extras: Fabric for front, back and trim of your choice. A printed silk with a pleated trim was used to make a 37 × 37 cm (14½ × 14½ in.) cushion
Cushion pad 38 × 38 cm (15 × 15 in.)

Notes: This design is most useful for using spare threads, as long as there is sufficient for a border and the background. Numerous colours can be used in the 'flames'.

Method

Work as described for the Fan cushion on page 74, but completing the square. The border chart has two narrow rows of diagonal satin stitches worked randomly. It is helpful to have a number of needles threaded with different colours. Work a few stitches in each colour, with varying distances between them. When the second row is worked the same way, the alignment of colour makes another pattern.

Adaptation: See Fan cushion (page 74) and Book cover (page 76).

Making up an inset panel

To fit embroidered inset ◇ shape

1 Cut out needlepoint with a 1 cm (½ in.) border.

2 Cut two pieces of fabric to the size required, including seam allowance.

3 Iron the fabric and lay one piece on a flat surface right side up.

4 Measure the halfway points along each side and mark with a pin pointing inwards.

5 Place the canvas *right side up* over the fabric with the corners lining up with the pins.

6 Tack in place with large stitches.

7 Turn the whole work over and smooth flat with an iron.

8 Mark round the ridge edge of the embroidery with a pencil.

9 Mark an inside turning of 2 cm (¾ in.) and cut out a small square.

10 Cut into corners carefully.

11 Fold back edges and press neatly to the edge of the embroidery. You are now looking at the back of your work, nicely padded with your couched ends and never to be seen by anyone else again!

12 Turn work over and undo tacking stitches.

13 Place the embroidery *under* the fabric – remembering not to turn either piece. The 'window' will fit round your work exactly.

14 With both canvas and fabric the right way up, tack into place before sewing together, using small stitches by hand or machine satin stitch. On the 'flame' cushion, two rows were considered most suitable as the silk would be fragile at the corners.

To fit embroidered inset □ shape
Use the method as for the ◇ shape, except at the following stages:

1 Measure the embroidery and mark the halfway points on each side with a pin facing inwards.

5 Line up the pins in the canvas with the pins in the fabric.

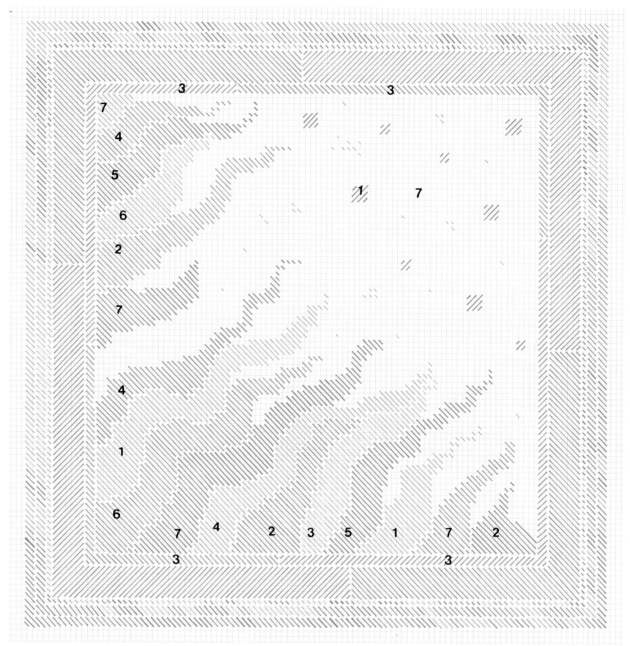

Flame cushion chart

Colour code		
1 Anchor 893	**4**	Anchor 847
2 Anchor 213	**5**	Anchor 778
3 Anchor 892	**6**	DMC 739
	7	DMC 746

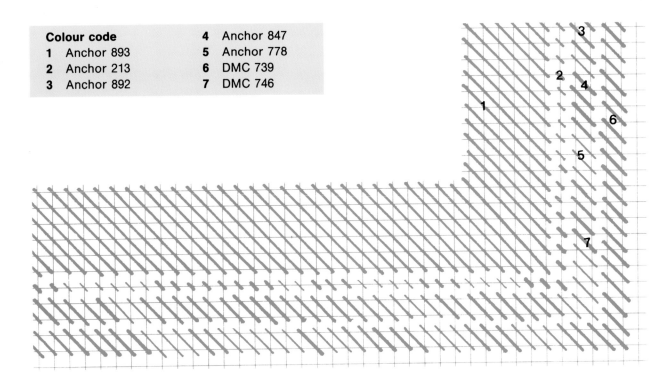

Colour code		4	Anchor 847
1	Anchor 893	**5**	Anchor 778
2	Anchor 213	**6**	DMC 739
3	Anchor 892	**7**	DMC 746

Border chart

Use the same method for inserting any shape. It works extremely well as long as each stage is followed with care.

Making up a cushion cover

1 Cut the fabric with 1 cm ($\frac{1}{2}$ in.) seam allowance.
2 Cut the canvas with 1 cm ($\frac{1}{2}$ in.) seam allowance around the embroidery and insert in fabric if the design requires it.
3 Prepare trimming – either covered piping cord or a fabric frill.
4 Sew to the right side of the front piece of fabric, rounding the corners slightly. If the front is all canvas, piping may not be necessary, and a square corner is determined by the pattern.

5 Place the front and back together with right sides facing.
6 Sew together leaving a 23 cm (9 in.) opening along one side.
7 Trim turnings and cut notches on any curves.
8 Turn inside out.
9 Ease in the cushion pad.
10 Turn the opening in neatly and ladder stitch together. As there is to be no frequent washing, a zip-fastener is unnecessary.

Notes: Ladder stitch gives a continuous thread that is easily pulled out when the cover has to be removed for dry-cleaning.

With embroidered corners it is advisable to stitch the backing fabric closely to the canvas and set the piping or trim only round the fabric part of the front.

FAN CUSHION

Charts: See page 72 and colour 1 of border chart on page 73
Fan cushion chart, see this page.
Dimensions: Sides 16 cm ($6\frac{1}{4}$ in.)
Canvas: 16's mono de luxe 20 × 20 cm (8 × 8 in.)
Yarns: One skein of each
Neon Rays Needlepoint Ribbon N94
Spring cotton and rayon 376
Ultra-suede U41 U33 U83
Eva Rosenstand embroidery floss 118 120
Needles: 18's and 20's tapestry
Extras: Organdie 108 × 56 cm (42 × 22 in.)
Fabric 50 × 100 cm (18 × 36 in.)
Piping cord 35 cm (14 in.)
Piece of toning fabric to cover piping cord
Cord for bow at base, made of cotton and rayon yarn
Cushion pad 40 × 40 cm (16 × 16 in.)
Notes: The yarns were all bought in the USA and used for fun with this pattern. The larger canvas combined with thicker threads gives an alternative set of textures to the 'flames'. Try your own selection of fancy yarns, with one colour but different textures.

Method

Mark an arc from the corner with sides 16 cm ($6\frac{1}{4}$ in.). Start in the corner and work outwards with the border. Avoid counting the border stitches by working a little at a time, returning to the 'flames'. Start these at the corner too and follow on either side, so that you only have to count one side as the other follows the hole previously used. Then work the background up to the arc marked.

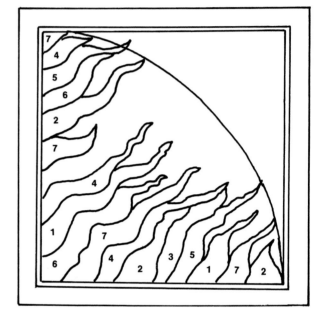

Fan cushion chart

Colour code
1 Neon Rays Needlepoint Ribbon N94
2 Spring cotton and rayon 376
3 Ultra-suede U41
4 Ultra-suede U33
5 ER/CW embroidery floss 118
6 Ultra-suede U83
7 ER/CW 120

ER/CW = Eva Rosenstand and Clara Weaver's stranded cotton

Fig 13a cord detail

Making up

1 Cut needlepoint with 1 cm ($\frac{1}{2}$ in.) canvas seam allowance and machine round close to work.

2 Fold the fabric in half to form a square, right sides together.

3 Draw an arc 42 cm (16$\frac{1}{2}$ in.) from one corner, and cut out fan shape. One piece forms the back of your cushion – place to one side.

4 Take the other piece and draw a small arc with sides 1 cm ($\frac{1}{2}$ in.) less than the needlepoint, and cut away this corner.

5 Machine stitch 1 cm ($\frac{1}{2}$ in.) inside both curved edges.

6 Cut organdie in half and join to form one long piece.

7 Attach it to the right side of the front fabric in very small pleats, along the longer stitched line.

8 Make large running stitches along the bottom edge and pull into a fan shape. It is longer than the fabric underneath so that the organdie can be held in place as you machine through the many layers just inside the stitched line.

9 Cut away excess organdie and cut into curve, up to stitched line.

10 Cover piping cord and cut up to stitched line.

11 Tack piping to curve of canvas work and tack the organdie-covered fabric over the same area. The cut edges will allow curving.

12 Machine through the three layers.

13 Machine the back and front together, right sides facing, following the line of the final row of needlepoint. Leave a gap at the top to insert cushion pad.

14 Trim corners and turn inside out. I found a square pad worked very well with one corner pushed inside itself to fill the curve.

15 Sew a cord to the base point and tie into a bow. I tied a knot on each thread and teased out the ends with a brush.

BOOK COVER

'Porthleven' by Jenny Edmonds.

This design is not fully charted.

I saw the print above at an exhibition and loved the vibrant colours. It is also a reminder of a large oil painting by the same artist which displayed the energy and movement typical of her work. The mono print by Jenny Edmonds was the starting point for a collection of yarns. Once I had started work with them they took on a jewel-like quality

far removed from the source material, which led to the addition of glass beads.

The book cover (see page 79) and following projects are built on colours that are nothing to do with interior decorating trends. Generally, when designing needlepoint for the home, the colours chosen will in some part link with their surroundings.

The idea of the book cover came from a commission. The original cover was for a *Book of Thoughts* with the words worked into the design, and the inside journal held in place with a matching cord.

Whatever size your book cover the arrangement is the same. Figure 14a gives the 'jewelled' squares which are used at the outside corners and on the inside border. The 'flames' from the chart on page 72 are set at the bottom edge and the repeat is set at the top edge. The gold area is adjusted to complete the shape. A cord edging is worked on the thread surrounding the embroidered canvas.

The background uses two shades of gold in irregular diagonal rows with some areas in 'flames' either of your own design or by following the chart turned upside down. If the 'flames' and some rows are worked in a lighter shade, this not only enhances the design but also gives markers to aim for. Is the phrase 'I will stop and go to bed when I get to that line' familiar to you?

There is space in the layout for a title or initials. Work them after the main pattern but before the background stitches. There are books of alphabets on canvas available if you need help. Stranded cotton is used throughout and you will need ample background colours. I used 10 skeins, and 1 skein of each of the main colours listed with the colour code, but the 'jewels' can be made from part-skeins with as many vibrant shades as you can find.

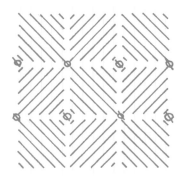

Fig 14a   'jewelled squares'

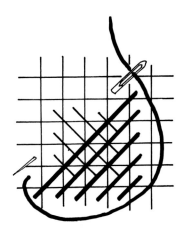

Fig 14b   double work each square

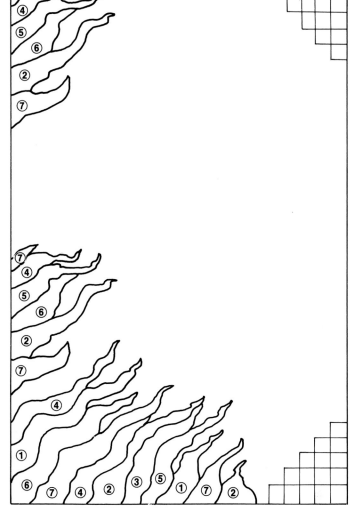

Book cover chart

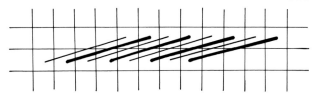

Fig 14c   stitch detail

Fig 14d   cord detail

Colour code

1	DMC 991	**7**	DMC 924
2	Anchor 212	**8**	Anchor 869
3	Anchor 210	**9**	DMC 550
4	Anchor 245	**10**	DMC 792
5	DMC 500	**11**	Anchor 119
6	Anchor 876	**12**	Anchor 874
		13	Anchor 886

'Jewelled' border
All the above colours plus:
Anchor 218 122 358
DMC 3328 975 738 937 793 943 315
A thimbleful of 'jewel'-coloured glass beads

1   Anchor 874
2   Anchor 886 (3 strands only)

WINDOW PELMET

The pelmet was an interesting project with the charts repeated to the size required, but the repeating of patterns is not my forté so the design developed with a compromise of having two patterns. Each one can be used in any permutation. The borders are separated to enable the size to be adapted. The entrance hall with its brightly painted green walls was an interesting start for the colour collection. The pelmet can be used above windows where curtains are not suitable. A needlepoint pelmet would look very interesting with plain curtains bordered in colours to match, but remember to choose the fabrics first and then match the yarns.

Charts: See pages 80–82

Dimensions: Each section is 23 × 10 cm (9 × 4 in.) Pelmet photographed is 60 cm (24 in.) long.

Canvas: 18's mono de luxe
Allow 5 cm (2 in.) border of canvas outside the area for needlepoint. If you wish to work on a larger-scale canvas, see page 16 for calculations to adapt.

Yarns: The quantities given are for each section, so multiples can be calculated.

Charts A and B	Charts C and D
DMC Medici wool	
8124 × 3	8124 × $3\frac{1}{2}$
8415 × 1	8415 × 1
8416 × 2	8416 × 1
Black × 1	Black × 1
Stranded cotton	
Anchor 228 × 1	228 × 1
873 × 1	873 × 2
109 × 1	109 × 1
230 × 1	230 × $\frac{1}{2}$
225 × 1	225 × $\frac{1}{2}$
853 × $\frac{1}{2}$	853 × $\frac{1}{2}$
DMC 309 × 1	309 × 2

Needles: 20's tapestry

Extras: Two pieces of wadding the size of the pelmet
One piece of stiffening the same size (there is a self-adhesive pelmet stiffener available)
Fabric for the backing
Sewing needle and thread to match
A strip of hook fastener the length of the pelmet

Notes: If a simple extension to the size is required, extend the side and carry the border up from the bottom. Work on a frame large enough to take the work in one piece; do not roll it up. If you are making a long pelmet, work in 60 cm (24 in.) sections and join them together. The design lends itself to this without any problems.

Method

1 See the photograph on pages 84 and 85 for details of working, and Figures 15a and 15b for close-up of rows. Figure 15e shows the layout.

2 I planned the 60 cm (24 in.) with the outside pattern divided in half; you will have to plan your own design to fit the situation. I would recommend starting in the middle of the top border and moving out to the sides.

3 Work the charts from the top downwards, with the large central designs completed before the background.

4 The border can be counted more reliably from near the large pattern, and once a border row has been set the others will follow. Always keep counting to the minimum.

5 The background tent stitches are not marked but the dots and clusters of tent stitches are worked before the background is completed, following the same direction.

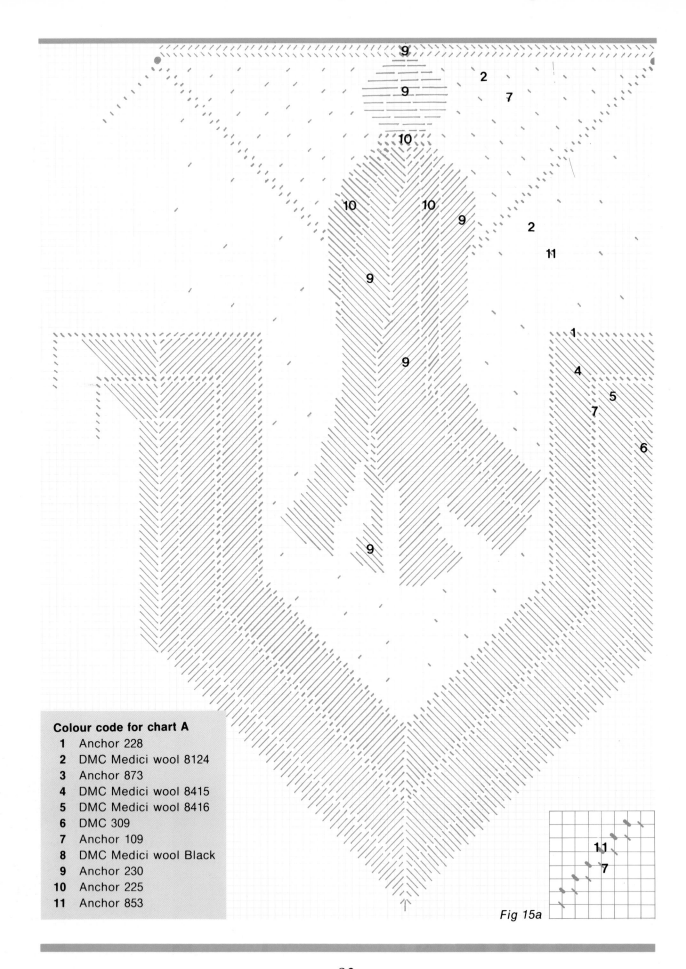

Colour code for chart A
1 Anchor 228
2 DMC Medici wool 8124
3 Anchor 873
4 DMC Medici wool 8415
5 DMC Medici wool 8416
6 DMC 309
7 Anchor 109
8 DMC Medici wool Black
9 Anchor 230
10 Anchor 225
11 Anchor 853

Fig 15a

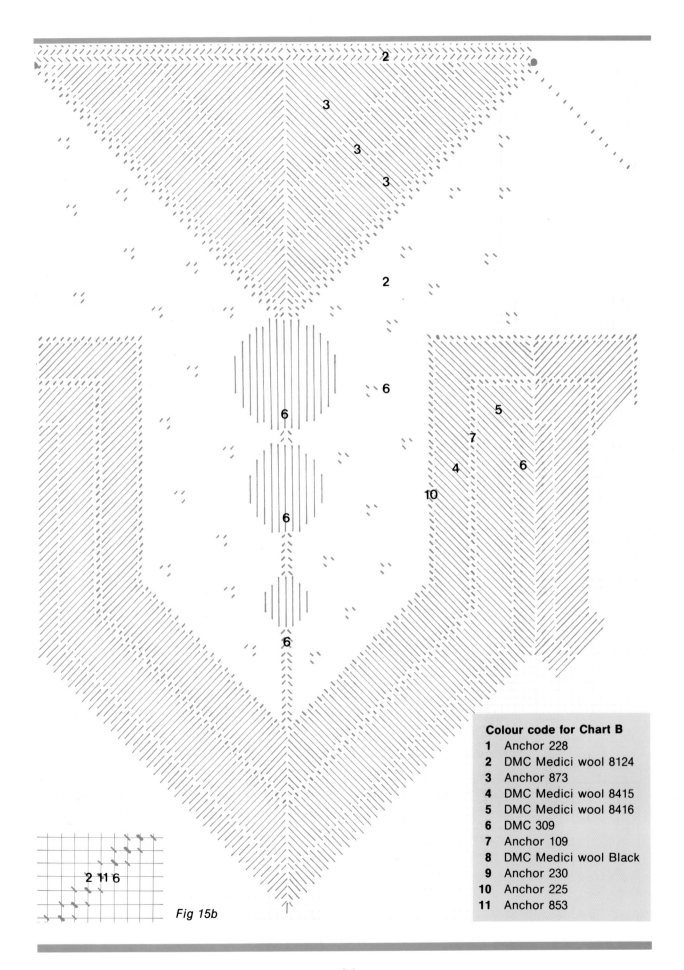

Fig 15b

Colour code for Chart B
1 Anchor 228
2 DMC Medici wool 8124
3 Anchor 873
4 DMC Medici wool 8415
5 DMC Medici wool 8416
6 DMC 309
7 Anchor 109
8 DMC Medici wool Black
9 Anchor 230
10 Anchor 225
11 Anchor 853

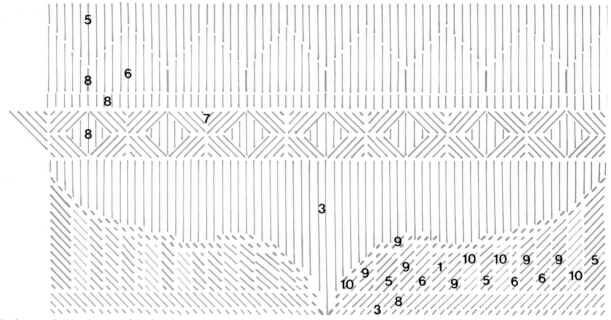

Window pelmet chart c: border

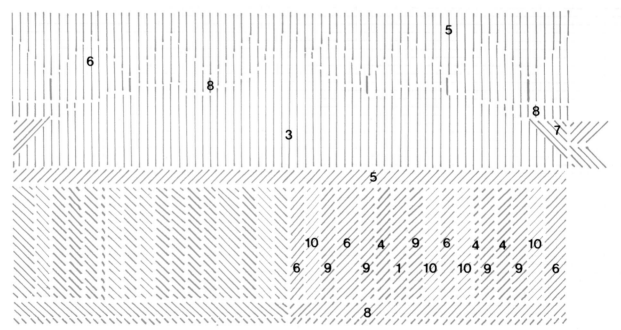

Window pelmet chart d: border

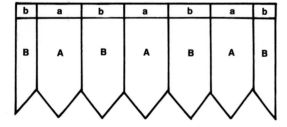

Fig 15e   plan showing window pelmet design

Making up

1 Cut a paper template exactly the size of your needlepoint.

2 The pelmet is put together in this order: canvas/wadding/stiffening/wadding/fabric/hook fastening.

3 Use the template to mark out the shapes but cut each one according to the instructions that follow.

4 Cut the needlepoint from the canvas with a 2 cm ($\frac{3}{4}$ in.) border.

5 Cut the wadding 1 cm ($\frac{3}{8}$ in.) inside the template line.

6 With a film of adhesive on the back of the embroidery, fix the wadding in place, just down the centre.

7 Cut the stiffening well inside the template line and place on the wadding, either with the sticky side down or with a film of adhesive enough to hold it in place.

8 A film of adhesive applied to the points of the canvas, sealing the embroidered edge, will help as you cut away the excess canvas very closely to get a good fit at the corners.

9 Fold all the canvas edges into place and press with an iron. If the stiffening is not cut small enough, the needlepoint will not fold far enough to the back and the backing fabric will come round the edges and be seen, which would be untidy, so trim if required.

10 Stick the remaining piece of wadding in place.

11 Cut the fabric with a 2.5 cm (1 in.) seam allowance at the top and sides but trim to 1 cm ($\frac{3}{8}$ in.) at the points.

12 Place over the back and tack into place, only through the wadding.

13 Fold the fabric under and ladder stitch to the embroidered edge, keeping the needlepoint over the edge with the fabric kept taut.

14 The front is held to the back with a few stitches set at regular points. A sewing cotton passed from the back and round a canvas thread and returned to be tied in a knot is efficient and neat. I used the meeting points of the two ogee shapes and the colour number 7 line in the bottom border.

Note on hanging: A strip of hook fastening was stitched to the back about 2.5 cm (1 in.) from the top. I put the loop side on the fabric and the hook side is stuck to a wooden batten which has flat fixing plates screwed to it; only two nails or hooks are required for the wall. This method is suitable for all lightweight hangings. The fastening allows quite subtle adjustments to be made to the level of the hanging, which is very helpful with older properties.

Adaptation: This design can be used for a wall tidy as described on page 86, or an exotic bed canopy in golds and creams. If the making up alarms you, the whole design could be made as a straight band with the area between the points completed in wide rows similar to those used in the curtain tie-back on page 64.

Overleaf: detail of window pelmet.

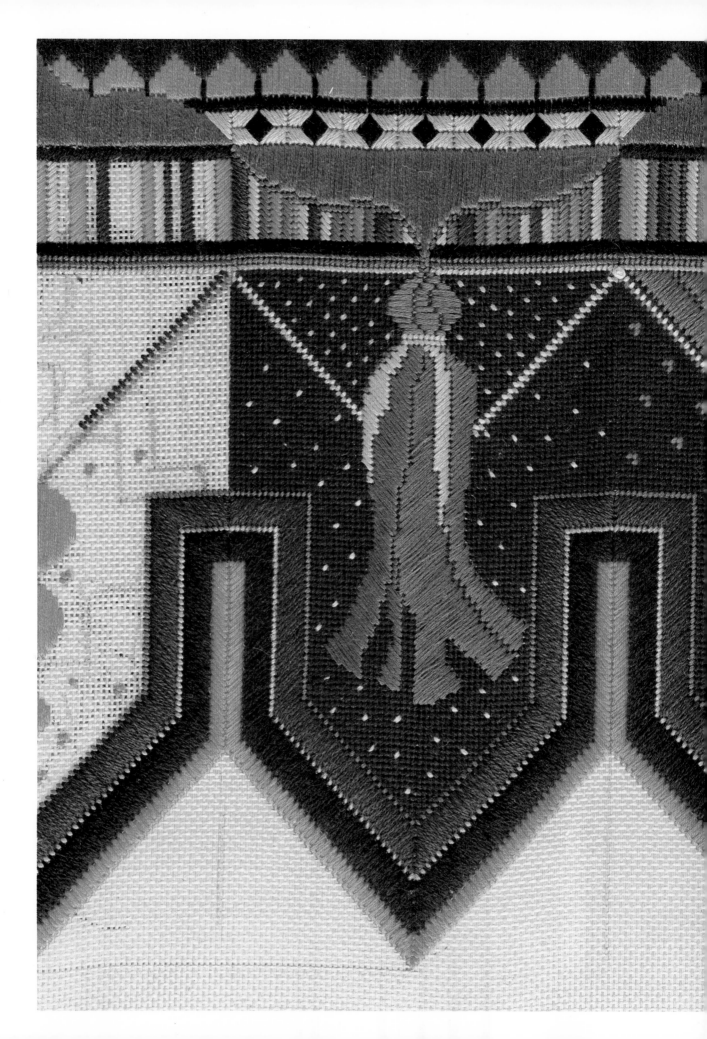

WALL TIDY

The greetings card below was sent to me in full knowledge that the picture's colour would excite. There are many such cards available, and reproduction technology allows artists' original work to reach more people. This striking pastel by Tony Hudson has strong areas of colour and gave me an excuse to use shades from the colour chart that had otherwise been neglected.

The wall hanging developed with the frivolous addition of a tassel. My preference for items with a function led me to divide the chart and to embroider two sections that were then joined as a pocket.

'Zulu Women' by Tony Hudson.

Charts: See page 88, also pages 81 and 82
Dimensions: 23 × 10 cm (9 × 4 in.)
Canvas: 18's mono de luxe 30 × 33 cm (12 × 13 in.)
Yarns: One skein of each unless otherwise stated
Stranded cotton
Anchor 891 307 326 123 109 400 89 × 2
DMC 322
Needles: 20's tapestry needle, sharp sewing needle
Extras: Fabric 30 × 50 cm (12 × 18 in.), three pieces 30 × 15 cm (12 × 6 in.)
Wadding 23 × 20 cm (9 × 8 in.), two pieces 23 × 10 cm (9 × 4 in.)

Perle yarn for tassel
Plastic tube for tassel (I used one found at an ironmonger's, for securing a screw)
Curtain ring
Large bead

Notes: Part of Chart D (page 82) is worked near the top of the canvas, and the area not worked forms the interlining. Chart B (page 81) forms the front of the wall tidy and is worked alongside Chart D set about 5 cm (2 in.) apart.

Method

1 Measure and mark out the two areas 23 × 10 cm (9 × 4 in.).

2 Note the shaping at the top and start at the centre of the chart on page 88 to set the outline. (Chart C on page 82 upside down might help you.)

3 Follow the pattern charts B (page 81) and D, noting the parts that are worked for the tidy.

4 Transfer to the right-hand side to work the front (see Figure 15b).

5 The groups of three tent stitches in a contrasting colour are quite random; work them before the background which, although not completed on the chart, is in tent stitch following the same direction.

Making up

1 Take the canvas from the frame and cut down the centre.

2 Join one piece of fabric to the straight edge of the embroidered back.

3 Join another piece of fabric to the top edge of the embroidered front. This is made up first.

4 Trim the embroidery, leaving a seam allowance of 1.5 cm ($\frac{3}{4}$in.) all round. (The fabric is still loose.)

5 Trim a piece of wadding to fit inside the shape and lightly stick to the back of the embroidery.

6 Press all canvas towards the back over the wadding, trimming the corners.

7 Press the fabric with a fold at the top edge and turn the seam allowances under to match the embroidered shape, trimming the corners.

8 Join the remaining edges together with ladder stitch and place to one side.

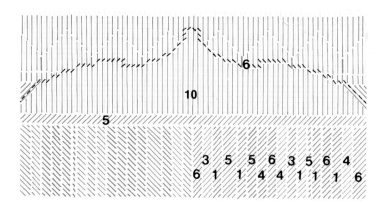

Wall tidy chart

6

10

5

3 5 5 6 3 5 6 4
6 1 1 4 4 1 1 1 6

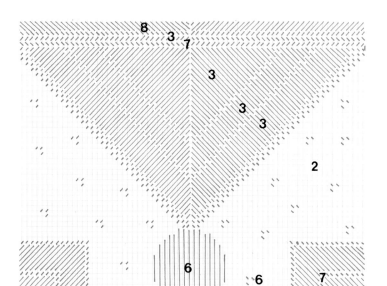

8 3
   7

3

3

3

2

6

6   6   7

6

4

6   10

5

6

6

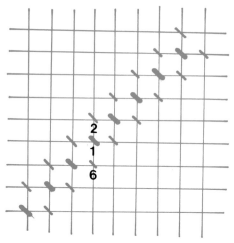

2

1

6

Fig 16a   stitch detail

Colour code
1 Anchor 891
2 Anchor 307
3 Anchor 326
4 DMC 322
5 Anchor 123
6 Anchor 89
7 Anchor 109
8 Anchor 400
9 —
10 Anchor 891

9 Take the back piece and press the fabric over the canvas and tack in place inside the marked area.

10 Trim with the same seam allowance, shaped at the top and straight at the base.

11 Lay the piece face down on the table and place the completed front on top, with the two embroidered edges meeting, and mark the outline on the canvas.

12 Cut a piece of wadding to fit inside the total area and fix in place with a little clear adhesive, making sure that none marks the fabric.

13 Trim the base rectangle to fit the pointed shape and press all seam allowances towards the back over the wadding.

14 Cut another piece of fabric to fit over the back, press the seam allowances in and ladder stitch the edge all round, covering all the canvas completely. Remove tacking stitches.

15 Place the completed front to the completed back and pin the bottom corners together while the sides are joined.

16 Use a toning yarn – three strands of cotton in a sharp needle is most suitable – and secure the top edges together of one side with two or three overstitches before herringbone stitching the front to the back. Take the needle through the backing fabric, and in a figure-of-eight movement loop the front embroidery and diagonally across to the back again about 1 cm ($\frac{3}{8}$ in.) from the previous stitch on each side.

17 Continue all round, making sure that the front is aligned with the back to finish at exactly the right spot. The stitching allows for continuous adjustment, so take a little care. It is an advantage if the front is slightly larger than the back to create a pocket, and the laced sides allow flexibility too.

18 Buttonhole stitch round a curtain ring and attach this to the top. The tassel is made with perle yarns and caught through the looped head with a long thread tied tightly in the middle. The plastic tube has a film of clear adhesive down one side and different lengths of coloured yarn are wound closely round, making sure the changing yarns are cut and secured over the adhesive. The tassel's long threads are then taken through the tube and through a large bead, which acts as a pivot; use both ends to make a few securing stitches at the point.

CURTAIN TIE-BACKS

It was the colour of the fabric shown below that attracted me. The artist Janosch designed the range of fabrics, and the choice of colours from the palette with the soft brushstroke pattern sets it apart from many textiles. For every shade he created, the fabric had to pass through the printing machine – no doubt a manufacturer's nightmare. It is much easier for the embroiderer to use colour like a painter. A simple but all too often overlooked solution is to use as many needles as colours. After using each colour, take the needle to one side of the work, bringing the needle from underneath and storing it on top of the canvas so that you know where it is.

I wanted the flower shapes to appear on either side of the 'ribbon' which would curve round the tie-back. This has not really happened but the band does set off the assorted coloured patterns very successfully.

The tie-backs were designed to fit the attic window. I wanted to achieve the sharp **W** shape at the top, so the measurements had to be precise. Paper was used to hold the curtains back and pinned to a satisfactory shape. A template is cut from this and used throughout the working and making up, so use a strong paper or thin card.

The design allows the background to be extended and flower shapes to be completed so that with a few adjustments it will fit the shape you need.

Charts: See page 92
Dimensions: 48 cm (19 in.) long, 2 cm ($\frac{3}{4}$ in.) at the narrow end and 7.5 cm (3 in.) at the widest end
Canvas: 18's mono de luxe 60 × 30 cm (24 × 12 in.)
Yarns: Stranded cotton, one skein of each unless stated otherwise
DMC 746 503 504
Anchor
213 214 117 848 158 847 869 871 292 × 5
295 × 9 894 893 892 × 2
Needles: 20's tapestry
Extras: Medium-weight iron-on Vilene 50 cm (18 in.)

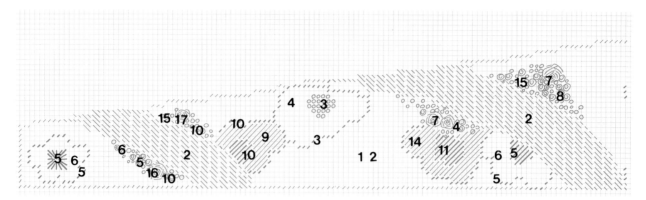

Curtain tie-backs chart A

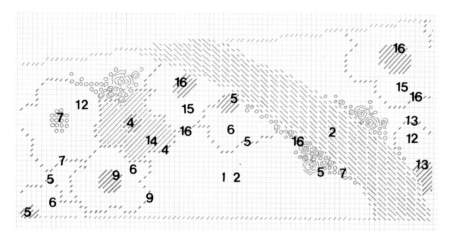

Curtain tie-backs chart B

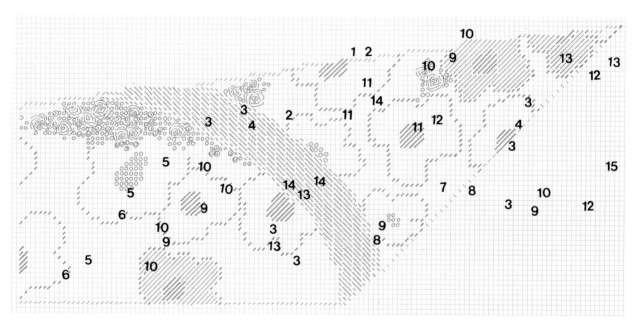

Curtain tie-backs chart C

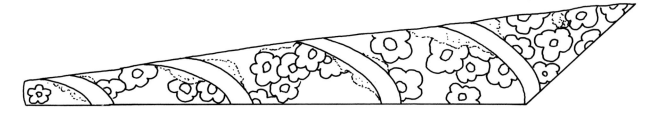

Fig 17d   layout of the design

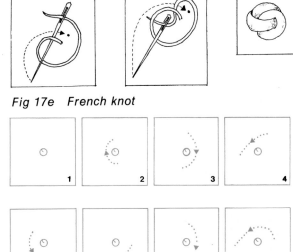

Fig 17e   French knot

Fig 17f   stitch guide for a rose

Fabric 36 × 123 cm (14 × 48 in.)
Wadding 25 × 50 cm (10 × 18 in.)
Sewing thread and needle
2 m (2 yd.) ribbon, cut into four equal lengths
Notes: Carrying the yarns in an irregular pattern across the back results in the canvas hole being covered. Avoid pushing through the hole and splitting the yarn, but move it to one side with the needle and couch over it. The finished needlepoint then has an even tension on the back and the front.

Start the matching tie-back by working the 'ribbons' in mirror image alongside the first set so that the canvas threads can be followed and the rows lined up more easily.

Use a fabric that does not fray easily, and preferably one that presses well. I used a rayon moiré fabric, but cotton chintz or dupion silk also complement needlepoint.

Method

1 Mark the halfway row of holes running lengthwise on the canvas. Place the template 1.5 cm ($\frac{3}{4}$ in.) to one side of the line and draw round the shape. Reverse the template and mark in the same way. The narrow gap is enough for the two pieces to be separated later.

2 This arrangement may not appear the most economical use of the canvas but it is practical as the chart has to be repeated in a mirror image. Use any lines marked on the canvas as guidelines only. Start with the outline of the 'ribbon' in tent stitch, going back to fill in the rows of longer stitches.

3 The chart shows the outline of the flowers in tent stitch, some of which are filled with long stitches. Where the grid is left uncharted, this is also worked in tent stitch in the numbered

The design has to be repeated in a mirror image when making a pair.

colour. The centres of each flower are in the same colour as the outline. There are clusters of 'roses', using the working method shown in Figure 17f. The ° are worked as french knots, some with a single wind of yarn and some double-sized with two winds of yarn round the needle.

4 For the background, I decided to work the tent stitches in the opposite direction to set off the pattern. The two shades of the same colour give a subtle tone. If space-dyed cottons were produced in softer colours they would be most useful, as the pattern developing from the shading gives interest and surprise to the worker. If there is a colour in the commercial range that suits your design, do consider using it. There are some overdyed yarns in America that have very pleasing shades. Whatever the yarn, work the background in diagonal rows of tent stitch, covering the canvas within the lines and up to all the 'flowers' and knots.

Adaptation: I have used part of the chart to produce a footstool, as seen on page 90.

Making up

NB The two pieces are not identical – there is a left and a right piece.

The tie-backs are made by bringing the backing fabric to the front and hemming next to the embroidery, while the other half of the tie is made in fabric and the two are joined at the front edge. Follow the stages carefully to avoid confusion. Keep all cut shapes together with the corresponding labelled templates.

1 Using the original template, label it (A). Cut two pairs from the wadding.

2 Place template (A) on firm paper or card and mark the shape plus a border of 0.5 cm ($\frac{1}{4}$ in.). Cut a template from this and label it (B).

3 Cut another shape with a border of 1.5 cm ($\frac{3}{4}$ in.) to make a template and label (C).

4 Cut the needlepoint from the canvas with a border of 0.5 cm ($\frac{1}{4}$ in.) and press lightly.

5 Cut two pairs of shape (B) from the Vilene.

6 Cut two pairs of shape (B) and one pair of shape (C) from the fabric.

7 Iron the corresponding shape of Vilene to the back of the embroidery with emphasis on the canvas edges.

8 Match a piece of wadding and with a film of clear adhesive down the middle of the Vilene, fix into place.

9 It is useful to work on the ironing table at this stage. Place a piece of (C) fabric wrong side up on the table, with the interlined canvas embroidery side up on the top.

10 The border of fabric has to be pressed with the iron over the canvas edge. This in turn is folded under and with neatly folded corners is hemmed to the outline stitch of the needlepoint.

11 Repeat this process for the other piece of needlepoint and the two fronts are complete.

12 The backs of the ties are also best organized on the ironing table. Place pairs of fabric right sides together on the table.

13 Match the shape of Vilene and iron into place.

14 With a film of clear adhesive, fix the wadding to the middle of the Vilene.

15 Press both pieces of fabric over the edge of the Vilene, giving a crease at the outside edge.

16 Slide the bottom piece of fabric out and place over the top of the wadding. If you reverse the fold, the line is clearly marked to handstitch front to back. Remember to trim the excess fabric at the corners.

17 Press all pieces before matching fronts to backs. Join the short pointed edges together with herringbone stitch.

18 A length of ribbon is attached at the 'eyelet' in the embroidery and another length at a matching point on the back. These are tied round the sides of the curtain rail.

FOOTSTOOL

In New Zealand I was introduced to an unusual yarn. The indigenous sheep and goats give fibres that produce an exciting yarn of wool and mohair. The lustre of the mohair gives an added dimension when it is dyed, as the s and z of the spinning take equal dye but the light catches the alternate directions of the worsted yarn, giving subtle shades.

As it was a new yarn I had to experiment to discover a suitable canvas. The crewel yarn used as a single thread works perfectly on an 18's mono canvas. With the stool, I wanted to achieve a textured look and used a single strand folded through the needle (against the normal maxim of all threads lying in the same direction). This worked very well on the 16's canvas and I am delighted with the result. The colours I chose were clear and reminiscent of an Auckland summer. They would have been ideal set against a white background but the grey/green was a more sensible choice for upholstery. A cushion worked with the white would be ideal for a seaside house.

The stool was custom-made with a shallow dome in order to display the pattern. Although the quantities given here relate to this stool, it is only the background quantity that needs adjusting. The plan for drawing on the canvas can be adapted for any size, placing the patterns in quarters. The smaller the stool, the nearer the knots of roses will meet in the middle. I realize that some will not have the 'Strands' yarn readily available and a substitute will have to be found, possibly strands of Paterna or that softest of yarns, Orchidee pure new wool. A stool cover is to last a lifetime, so use the best yarns available.

Charts: A and B, see page 92
Dimensions: Upholstered base diameter 30 cm (12 in.)
Embroidery 38 cm (15 in.) diameter

Canvas: 16's mono de luxe 50 × 50 cm (19 × 19 in.)
Yarns: 'Strands' wool and mohair, pure New Zealand crewel yarn, one skein of each colour unless otherwise stated
Background 414 × 42 (used double) 514 494 493 451 043 153 385 391 323 393 433
Needles: 20's tapestry
Notes: I know there is a lot of boring background, but I wanted the colours to have space. The colour is broken by changing the direction of the yarn and also by using larger stitches.

Colour code

		(1)	(2)	(3)	(4)
1		433	433	—	153
2		514	514	514	514
3		494	393	493	493
4		493	391	153	494
5		451	451	433	385
6		043	043	385	391
7		153	494	323	043
8		385	323	451	393
9		391	493	494	433
10		323	153	043	323
11		393	385	493	451

Background 414

Small motif

For the chart numbers shown in (1), replace with corresponding colours as listed:

(1)	(2)	(3)	(4)
9	10	14	4
7	1	11	7
9	10	14	4
12	14	1	11
1	9	8	12
1	9	8	12

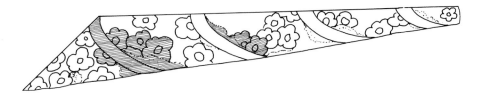

Fig 18b   shaded areas for footstool design

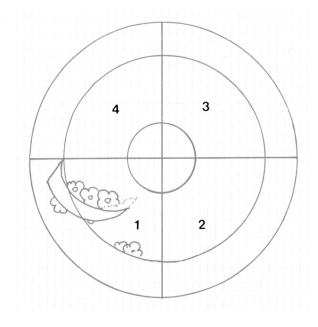

Fig 18a   layout

Fig 18c   centre circle stitch detail

Method

1 Mark the canvas with a line through the centre in both directions.

2 Draw a circle 38 cm (15 in.) in diameter by marking points 19 cm (7½ in.) from the central point at frequent intervals.

3 Draw another circle 33 cm (13 in.) in diameter.

4 Draw another circle 10 cm (4 in.) in diameter.

5 Use the areas shaded in Figure 18b; see Charts B and C on page 92.

6 Place the large motif charted in A on page 92 on the canvas at the junction of the line and middle circle (see Figure 18a).

7 Work the parts of the charts as colour code on each marked quarter of the canvas.

8 The small motif from chart A on page 92 is worked on the middle circle between, the large patterns. A precise placing is not important.

9 Work as in the Figure 18c with rows of stitches worked in the opposite direction from the remaining tent-stitched background.

10 Trim the canvas to a circle and mount over the upholstered stool top. Fix the base from the bottom. No trimming is required.

Adaptation: This design can be made into a round cushion, working an area 23 cm (9 in.) in diameter to set into fabric.

An 18's mono canvas de luxe takes 'Strands' crewel wool and the Eva Rosenstand stranded cotton range as complementary colours — a blue background with pinks.

'Strands' 171 173 172 011 201

Eva Rosenstand 233 238 121 113 122 124

FRIVOLOUS CUSHION

The tactile qualities of ribbons and the intricacy of pattern in lace are reasons enough for the embroiderer to include them in her collection. With nostalgic associations too they provide additional trimmings to pretty items. I incorporate ribbons in many of my designs. Couched velvet ribbons were used with wool and cotton for an upholstery fabric seen on the chair on page 124, which gives a rich and tailored appearance.

The cushion also has couched velvet ribbons, but the satin ribbons and lace are stitched directly to the canvas by different methods (see Figure 19a).

The ribbons can run right over the edge of the canvas or be included within a border. The border is worked last and a sharp needle used to pierce through the ribbons into the canvas hole below with an allowance of ribbon held neatly underneath the border.

Imagination and dexterity applied to familiar materials create a cushion panel that is delightfully decorative. The 'Frivolous cushion' is not as silly as it sounds, for the project gives the embroiderer an opportunity to display a variety of talents. I have set the title as a project with students who have produced some beautiful pieces of work, and I have learnt from them some of the reasons for its success. It is a small project which increases the optimism about completing it, and as the ribbon covers square centimetres of the canvas so quickly, the time 'saved' can be applied to the detailed embroidery which is concentrated in small areas. There are quite a few ideas given here but let your imagination take over.

Chart: See page 100
Dimensions: Chart 18 × 18 cm (7 × 7 in.)
  Total 25 × 25 cm (10 × 10 in.)
Canvas: 18's mono de luxe 35 × 35 cm (14 × 14 in.)

Yarns: Stranded cotton, one skein of each unless stated otherwise
DMC Ecru × 3 739
Anchor 847 858
DMC Medici wool 1505A 509 120B
Lacemaking thread, or a similar fine, smooth yarn
Needles: 20's tapestry, beading needles
Extras: Packet of small white beads
Packet of grey beads
Thimbleful of gold glass beads
Thimbleful of mother-of-pearl glass beads
2 metres (yd.) of lace 8 cm (3 in.) wide
1 metre (yd.) of narrow (3 mm) double-sided satin ribbon
Cushion pad 25 × 25 cm (10 × 10 in.)
Backing fabric 30 × 30 cm (12 × 12 in.)
Notes: The chart overleaf records only one corner of the central pattern completed. Repeat on all four corners. Figure 19a shows the application of ribbon and lace for the border as seen opposite. The background stitches are only indicated to allow the pattern to be seen more clearly. See page 27 for details of beading.

Method

1 Measure and mark the shape on the canvas as a guide.
2 Mark the centre thread in each direction.
3 Start with the middle square which is interwoven threads. With six strands of colour number 3, bring the yarn up eight threads above the centre and bring it down over sixteen threads and work in a long satin stitch to complete the square with seven more stitches either side of the first.
4 Coming through the canvas at the holes marked at the sides, weave the yarn over three

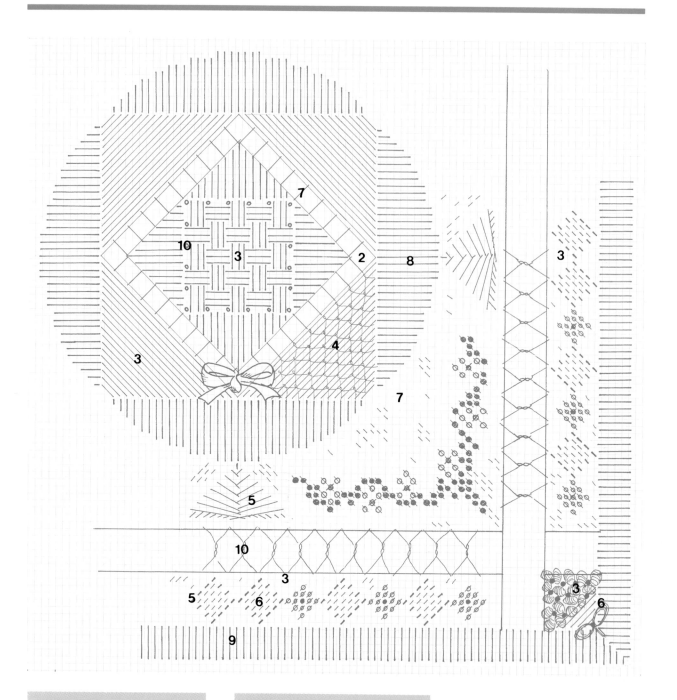

Colour code
1 Velvet ribbon
2 Satin ribbon
3 DMC 739
4 Lace thread
5 Anchor 847
6 Anchor 858
7 DMC Ecru
8 DMC Medici wool 505
9 DMC Medici wool 509
10 DMC Medici wool 120B

Key
✗ Gold glass bead
○ French knot
✦ Grey bead
🐚 Bullion knot
🕸 White bead
● Mother-of-pearl glass bead

Frivolous cushion chart

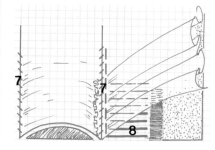

Fig 19a   sewing lace and ribbons

Fig 19b   French knot

and under three long stitches in groups of three as charted. This is all on the surface of the canvas.

5 Work colour number 10 and return to work the french knots at the edges as charted.

6 Leave the rows for the ribbon until after completing the next stage.

7 Work colour number 3 in long diagonal stitches as charted and then cover with number 4 in the following way, working loosely to give the shape. Bring the needle through at the third longest row and loop it through the canvas thread at the point shown. Repeat until the end where the needle goes down at the third row and comes up at the sixth row to return along the row, hooking the needle round the loops above in a buttonhole stitch manner. Continue this method to the corner and repeat on the other corners.

8 Work the circle as the chart, counting carefully.

9 The pattern worked by colour number 5 absorbs the spare thread that runs through the centre of the design. Start at the outside long diagonal stitch, pass across two threads at the back and come down diagonally on the opposite edge. Adapt the angle and number of threads as you repeat the pattern to the chart. Note the little extra straight stitch at the top that completes the 'arrow head'.

10 The areas between the 'arrow heads' have the direction of stitches marked and the beads applied in the same direction.

11 The velvet ribbon is couched with a single strand of wool which is worked in a loose straight couching stitch, but each alternate one is looped twice round the previous straight yarn adding a lacy appearance but holding the ribbon firmly in place.

12 Work the beaded border next. The white beads surround a gold bead on one side, and a mother-of-pearl bead is central on the other side. The opposite borders will match when completed.

13 Secure the velvet ribbon under the straight stitches of the final border on the chart opposite.

14 In the outer corner, work clusters of french knots and bullion stitch, and add a few beads to make 'bunches of flowers'. Some stitches appearing as 'stems' come from the 'flowers' to the corner and are wrapped together with colour number 6 and tied in a bow.

15 The panel can be used like this, or the frilly border as shown in Figure 19a can be added.

16 The satin ribbon is stitched along its selvedge to the canvas. In the example shown, a strip of wadding was laid underneath – as this alters the number of threads covered, do check the number that suits your work rather than make it fit the chart.

17 The outer border is worked next.

18 The lace is then applied between rows as detailed in Figure 19a. The details of machine stitching and fabric are also indicated.

Outer borders: When joining the backing fabric to the needlepoint, remember to keep the outside edges free from ornament as that would hinder a neat finish. An interesting row of beads at the edge causes chaos on the machine, as does a bundle of lace too close to the outside. The border, covering five to seven threads, serves to support the lace and frames the panel instead of falling away over the edge, so is a practical feature.

Making up

See cushion-making on page 73.

Adaptation: The central circle can be used, with a variation in the centre, as a box top. This chart does not transfer well to a different canvas.

SEWING TRAY COVER

The sewing tray was born out of a need to see my sewing equipment at a glance and to stop wasting time rummaging in deep baskets. The padded cover was decorated with inset triangles of needlepoint in pretty pastel shades. I still have baskets littering the workroom, but each has its growing collection of materials for another project, and seems perfectly workmanlike. The tray was to be beautiful as well as practical.

I have acquired a selection of yarns, silks and organdie that 'came in useful' for this project.

The plain wooden tray was painted pastel yellow with turquoise edging and the sides had a diagonal zig-zag marked in the glaze, barely perceptible.

A padded silk liner was made, the pocket in one corner, and all the edges were trimmed in layers of zig-zag organdie.

This small pocket for a pair of scissors, and the pretty pincushion, have been made in the same pastel shades for use with the sewing tray.

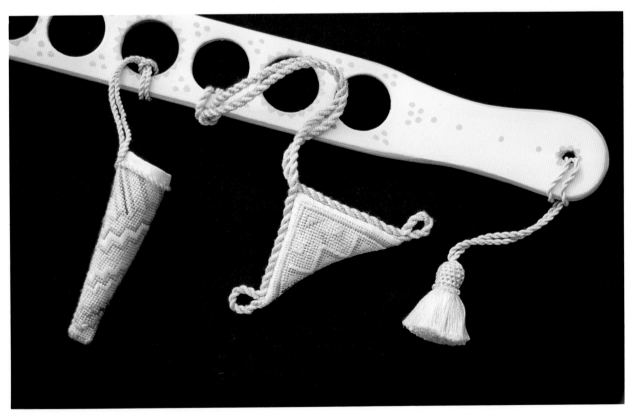

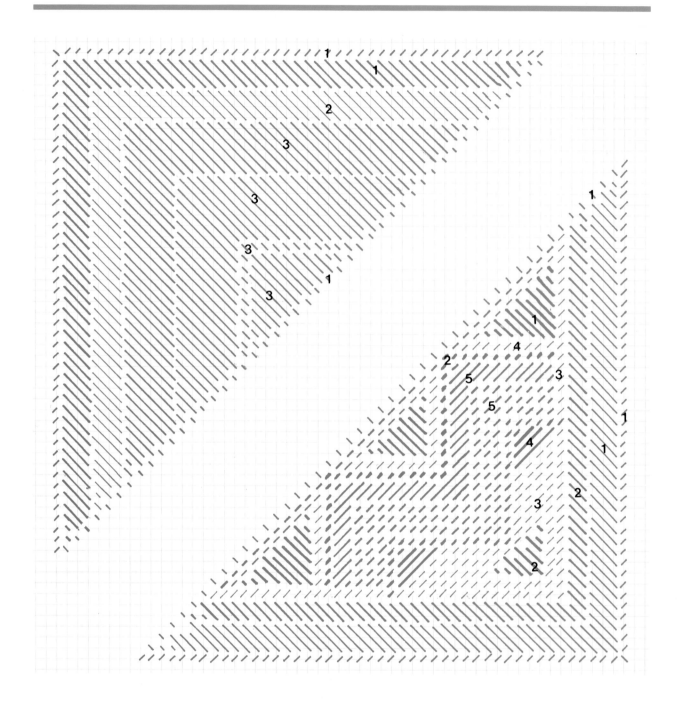

Colour code

1	DMC 745	**3**	Anchor 880
2	Anchor 167	**4**	DMC 745
		5	DMC 747

Sewing tray cover charts
Top left corner: A
Bottom right corner: B

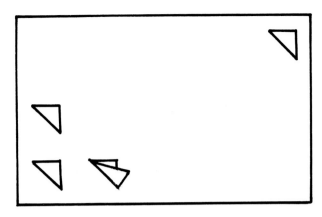

Fig 20a   layout for sewing tray

Fig 20b   French knot

Fic 20c   cord detail

INSETS AND TABS

I have worked corners of cushions as seen on page 114. These are simply triangles and once isolated and the site determined they can be worked in a number of ways. The inset method used on the sewing tray cover on page 102 lends itself to cushions just as well, but cut away the excess canvas.

If the triangle is backed with fabric it makes a tab that can be used on wall hangings as a decorative feature or as a useful lifting device. Double-sided triangles make pincushions (see page 103 and detail page 107), and if left folded and flat with a cord and tassel attached to the point they make lovely bookmarks.

Chart: See opposite

Dimensions: Each triangle 7 × 7 × 10 cm (3 × 3 × 4 in.)

Total 50 × 35.5 cm (19½ × 14 in.)

Canvas: 18's mono de luxe 60 × 46 cm (24 × 18 in.) plus 15 × 15 cm (6 × 6 in.) for the lifting tab

Yarns: Pure silk would maintain the quality but this cover is worked in stranded cotton. One skein of each colour unless stated otherwise

DMC 747 754 745 × 2

Anchor 880 × 2 167

Needles: 20's tapestry

Extras: Dupion silk fabric for the top and backing, 60 cm (¾ yd) length

Lightweight polyester wadding 50 × 35.5 cm (19½ × 14 in.)

Clear adhesive

Sewing needle and matching thread

Notes: The canvas acts as the stiffening for the cover, so keep it as flat as possible. The canvas requires a border so that the shape will not be distorted when mounted on the frame; do not roll but use a larger frame if necessary. The fabric must be cut on the straight, the warp and weft matching the direction of that on the canvas.

The measurements apply to a specific tray but they are adaptable to any size.

Method

1 Measure the size of the tray top and mark out accurately on the canvas as this will be the cutting line.

2 Decide where to place the triangles and which one is to have the lifting tab.

3 Note the layout in Figure 20a and work from the chart opposite.

4 Work the tab as Chart B on a *separate* piece of canvas.

Making up

To make the tab

1 Cut the small triangle with a 1 cm (½ in.) border of canvas.

2 Place a thin film of clear adhesive on the back and let it dry.

3 Cut a piece of silk the same size; with the right sides facing, back stitch the straight sides together.
4 Trim across the top corner and turn inside out, pushing the point into shape very carefully. Press the tab, making sure the fabric is well to the back.
5 Tack the base edges together. Keep until stage 12.

To make the cover

6 Place a piece of wadding over the total area. A little clear adhesive near the edges will keep it in place.
7 Cut out the triangles a little larger than the needlepoint underneath.
8 Cut the fabric to size with a seam allowance and tack into place over the wadding.
9 Cut out the triangles 1 cm ($\frac{1}{2}$ in.) smaller than the embroidered shape. To do this insert sharp scissors over the triangle area, and locate the exact shape through a very small hole.
10 To turn in the seam allowance the fabric has to be cut exactly into the corners. Good scissors are essential.

11 Turn under the edges and stitch through fabric and canvas with tent stitches. Apply fabric to all triangles except the one for the tab. See advice on fabric sewing on page 113.
12 To attach the tab, place it on top of the cover triangle. Tack the base edges under the wadding then tack into place.
13 Although the tab conceals your view, a peep underneath allows you to see the line of holes for a row of diagonal tent stitches through all the layers. Line up the two triangles and, with the fabric folded over the wadding, stitch securely with an extra stitch at the corners.
14 Cut the canvas from the frame, trimming it to the correct size.
15 Press the top fabric over the edge of the canvas onto the back.
16 Tack the backing into place and press the seam allowance underneath.
17 Join the edges together invisibly, adding any trim at this stage. Corner pieces made from extra organdie can be added, and ribbons tie the cover to the handle of the tray at one end.

PINCUSHION

Charts: See page 104
Dimensions: 5 × 5 × 7 cm (2 × 2 × 2¾ in.)
Canvas: 22's mono canvas 9 × 9 cm (3½ × 3½ in.)
Yarns: As for sewing tray cover. Use three strands throughout
Needles: 22's tapestry
Extras: Soft fibre or wool filling
2 sewing needles and matching thread
Notes: A piece of canvas about 20 × 20 cm (8 × 8 in.) mounted on a small frame is portable for travelling. Setting yourself a number of small projects within the area increases the chance of completing at least one of them while on holiday. Work the same pattern in a permutation of colours so that none is identical – one for you and one for a friend.

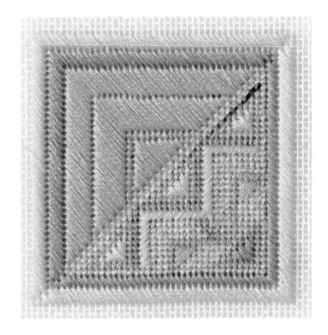

Method

Work the charts A and B on page 104 without any space between them.

Making up

1 Cut the embroidery with a 1 cm (½ in.) border of canvas.
2 Fold the embroidery in half with the wrong sides together. Trim the seam allowance across the top point and taper towards the side points.
3 Have a needle threaded for each side, and overstitch the turned-in canvas edge. Work a little at a time from each point while pushing the filling into place firmly as you go. Secure at the top.
4 The finishing requires some dexterity and does not make a very neat edge, but the application of a cord to cover the seam and to continue as a hanging loop provides a practical decoration. See page 103.

Adaptation: Pincushions can be made with either of the two patterns backed with fabric like the tab, or each chart can be reversed to complete a square. They can be worked on any size canvas and can provide patterns for inset cushion fronts.

SUGAR ALMONDS CUSHION

This design idea is not charted.

The cushion has a border surrounding rows of straight stitches, velvet and satin ribbons and fine organdie applied over part of the work. Random heaps of 'almonds' reveal its source.

The 'sugar almonds' design was worked on 18's mono canvas with Appletons tapestry wools 851, 752, 602, 101, 991 and 705, and stranded cotton in the following colours: Anchor 893, 109 and 869, DMC 225 and Ecru. Choosing the colours that please is the most important design decision before deciding the order of working. If the almonds are to be worked, place the group on a line and complete them before the surrounding rows, using stranded cotton as indicated on this page.

If ribbons are to be added, see Figure 19a for the technique and note that the ends have to be fixed under the border stitches.

The border is the same as on page 112, using Appletons wools and Anchor stranded cotton – see the colour code and chart on page 113.

This cushion was backed with a glazed cotton, and as the border dictated the edge and the shape, no piping was used and the corners were kept square. See page 73 for making up cushions. **Straight stitches** worked in rows over any number of canvas threads is the simplest of designs and is effective as well as rewarding for the beginner.

Colour code
1 Appletons tapestry wool 601
2 Appletons tapestry wool 991
3 Appletons tapestry wool 752
4 Appletons tapestry wool 101
5 Anchor 869
6 Appletons tapestry wool 851

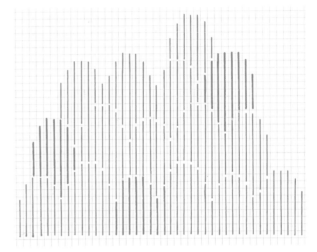

Fig 21a   detail of 'sugar almonds'

Colour code
1 Anchor 109   3 Anchor 869
2 DMC 225   4 DMC Ecru

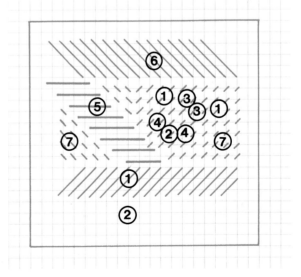

Fig 21b   detail of border

109

CUSHION CORNERS AND BORDERS

Border and leaves (see cushion page 114)
These design ideas are not fully charted.

Chart: See opposite (plus leaves)

Dimensions: Sides 24 cm (9½ in.) for 40 × 40 cm (16 × 16 in.) cushion

Canvas: 18's mono de luxe

Yarns: One skein of each unless stated otherwise. Only three of the following colours are used in the border.
Appletons tapestry wool 991 123 223
DMC stranded cotton Ecru 503 × 4 504 738
Anchor stranded cotton 894 893 858 848

Needles: 20's tapestry

Extras: Medium crewel needle
Fabric for making up, two pieces 43 × 43 cm (17 × 17 in.)

Notes: This design was developed after seeing an upholstery fabric on a 1930s chair on exhibition at a Budapest art gallery.
The background also has a small pattern, which is worked in the opposite direction before the main colour stitches. When working corners, match the major colour to the fabric so that they blend comfortably together. If the inside edge of the border is worked first, there is an edge to work your next design against, reverting to the repeated border in between. This keeps both your interest and the canvas growing together.

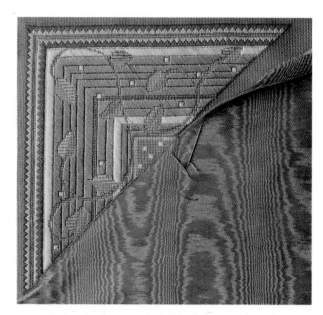

Method

Decide on the size you want the corner. The easiest way to judge is to start a piece of the border; here a line of tent stitch was started at the corner and worked in each direction. Do the same until it fits your idea. Draw the desired pattern, remembering to make use of tools. So often the wish to get started means that we actually make things difficult for ourselves by not using the best equipment. Specific shapes can be found at a graphic art shop, but curves, set-squares and compasses from a local stationer's can all help to reproduce an identical curve. Try cutting one pleasing shape that you can use as your template – it is the identical repetition of such shapes that gives a professional touch to a piece of work.

Work the 'stem' lines first, followed by the leaves then the background squares, and the main background to finish. All the time sew more of the border. Keep the stitches near the fabric edge as suitable as possible for a neat join (see above).

Making up

See page 73 for making up a cushion cover.

Adaptation: Work this as a whole cushion, with the area of leaves forming an inner border and the central part made up of more little squares with a tent stitch background.

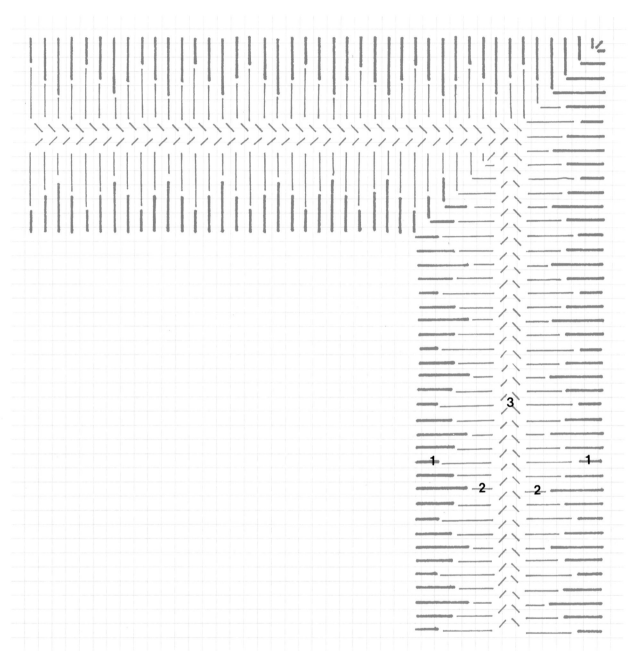

Cushion corner border chart

Colour code

1 Appletons tapestry wool 123
2 Appletons tapestry wool 223
3 DMC 503

Border and flowers (see cushion page 114)

Chart: See opposite

Dimensions: Sides 23 cm (9 in.) for 40 × 40 cm (16 × 16 in.) cushion

Canvas: 18's mono de luxe

Yarns: One skein of each unless stated otherwise. Not all the colours are used in the border. Appletons tapestry wool 851 223 752 123 991 DMC stranded cotton 503 × 2 Ecru 504 738 Anchor stranded cotton 893 × 2 858 848 894 758 892

Needles: 20's tapestry

Extras: Medium crewel needle Fabric for making up, two pieces 43 × 43 cm (17 × 17 in.)

Notes: The pattern co-ordinates furnishing fabrics used in a sitting-room. Any shapes can be drawn on the canvas as long as the areas are small enough to fill in with threads of a practical length – too long and they will snag. Tapestry wool worked on the straight, or in diagonal long stitch, is ideal on 18's canvas but is too thick for tent stitch, when it would be necessary to use strands of crewel wool.

Method

Work the border from the chart opposite. Remember that if you start from the corner the size can be adjusted. Work the colours in the order they are numbered and remember the tight fit when working the 'ribbon' with back stitches, filling in the background with stranded cotton.

The pattern needs to be drawn with a fine pen. Work an outline, remembering to keep the stitches in the same direction to save problems. Keep the stitches near the fabric edge lying in the same direction so that the join can be sewn as neatly as possible and embroidery and fabric merge (see photograph on page 110).

Making up

See page 73 for making up a cushion cover.

Adaptation: Make a full cushion square on 14's mono canvas by using this border and adding half of the Cushion corner (page 110), either inside or outside. Complete the middle either with your own design or with the 'Basket of Fruit' from page 36.

Cushion border chart.

Applying fabric to corner canvas

With the moiré fabric used in photograph, the stranded cotton was divided and three threads seemed suitable. It is important to consider the weight and texture of fabric when deciding how thick to use the cotton. Sometimes the round appearance of six strands gives a positive neat edge that completes the design.

Colour code
1 Appletons tapestry wool 991
2 Anchor 893
3 Appletons tapestry wool 123
4 Appletons tapestry wool 223
5 Appletons tapestry wool 752
6 Appletons tapestry wool 851
7 DMC 503

Method

1 Keep the canvas on the frame, even if you have embroidered another piece on the same canvas.

2 Take the square of fabric and lay right side up over the work, leaving an overlap of 1 cm ($\frac{1}{2}$ in.) for the hem.

3 Fold back the corner of fabric to reveal the embroidery and with the fingers press the crease to line up precisely halfway across the stitches in the last diagonal line (see page 110).

4 Leave 2 cm (1 in.) past the crease for a hem and trim away the fabric corner.

5 With cotton threaded in the crewel needle, secure thread underneath. If you start in the centre it will hold the fabric in position.

6 Bring the needle up through the canvas and stitch hole and *down* into the fabric to give another diagonal row of tent stitches (see page 110).

7 It is more difficult to see at the border where there are straight stitches but you will have developed a regular spacing technique as you sewed. This is a difficult manoeuvre but you can peep under the fabric to locate the hole as you go along (which is why tacking is not recommended).

SMALL MIRROR FRAME

The small mirror frame continues the theme of ideas which assist with the transition to individual designs (see page 102). Some ideas have charts that are without colour coding, some have parts charted, and there are ideas for you to follow through on your own. It is very much a matter of decision-making, and the more confident you are the easier it is. This confidence builds when there is approval of what you have achieved from others. More important though, is the confidence gained when *you* feel something has worked satisfactorily. I suggest you combine charted work with a piece of your own design so that you can more easily visualize the finished appearance. Some people prefer the relaxation of repetition in needlepoint, without the need to make more decisions; for these there are a number of charts to put together to made individual combinations of pattern and colour.

Those wishing to draw their own patterns should use a fine waterproof pen. Specialist embroidery shops have suitable fabric pens, and graphic art shops have large selections of spirit-based felt pens in lovely colours and shades for filling in coloured areas or tinting your canvas. Do not be tempted to use too much detail at this stage, but let the needle and thread be the best guide to the developing pattern. This will allow you to change your mind and work that last inspiration.

Charts: See pages 116 and 117 (not colour coded)
Dimensions: Border 3.5 cm ($1\frac{3}{4}$ in.)
Total 24 × 19 cm ($9\frac{1}{2}$ × $7\frac{1}{2}$ in.)
Canvas: 18's single de luxe 35 × 30 cm ($13\frac{1}{2}$ × 12 in.)
Yarns: One skein of each unless otherwise stated
Anchor stranded cotton 842 264 848 158 852 885 926 276 4146 (Cord) 264 885
Needle: 20's tapestry

Extras: Kits are available to make free-standing mirrors. If not, the materials needed are:
Acid-free card
Polyester wadding to pad the frame
Cord for the inside edge (if not handmade)
6 mm ($\frac{1}{4}$ in.) wide velvet ribbon for the outside edge
Notes: The colours used are all muted and can be used in any combination successfully on this pattern. I have continued the colours of the straight border round the outer edge interspersed with areas of diagonal stitching in assorted shades. If you are uncertain about the quantity of yarn for the work, divide it into sewing lengths and then into four bundles. This will enable you to distribute it evenly through the work without running out on one part and leaving it unbalanced.

Method

Start by lightly marking the area to be stitched on your canvas using the kit template if you have one. Use this as a guide only and start the outside border which will use most of one colour. Put the smaller pattern stitches in the border before you reach them with the bands.

Making up

Follow the instructions on page 54 for making a hanging mirror if you are unable to find a suitable kit.

Adaptation: Worked in shades of cream and white with a little gold thread, this design would make a very pretty photograph frame for a wedding present.

115

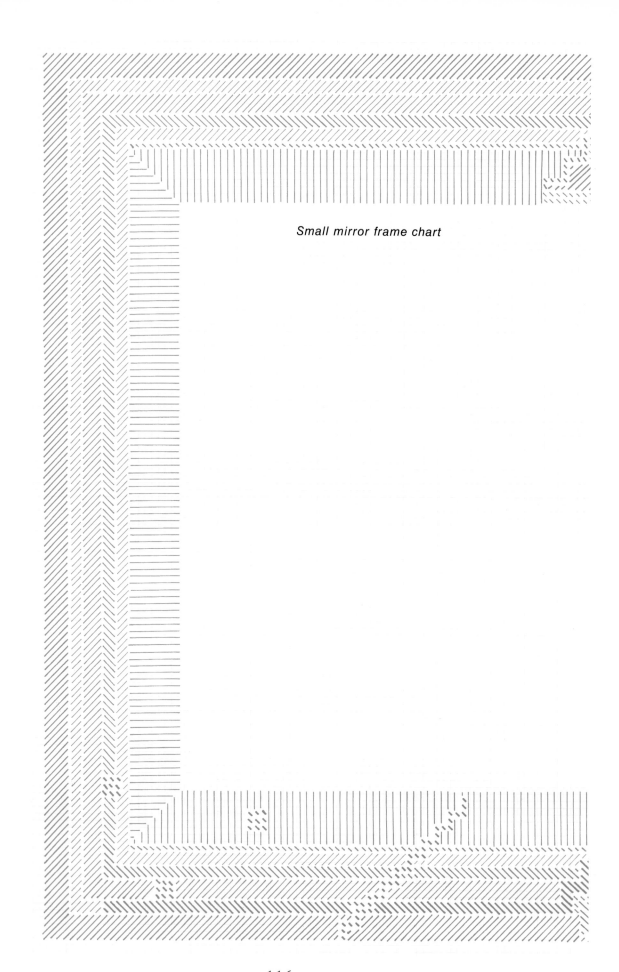

Small mirror frame chart

KILIM DESIGNS

The kilim is only one of many types of rug in oriental carpet displays. The richness of fibres and dyes reflect their history and geography. The nomadic journeys, economic restrictions and political changes are all interwoven to contribute to the continued fascination with carpets way beyond the 'fashionable' label given them by the interior decorator.

The kilim can be any non-pile carpet, the most familiar being Turkish or Persian. The Indian equivalent is known as a dhurrie, with quite different colours.

The structure of the woven shapes suggests patterns that are ideally suited to canvas work. Making copies is no substitute for the real thing; the important thing is to use wool, colour and texture in such a way that they remind you of the rugs.

A detail of the kilim designs shown opposite.

A corner of the study in the picture opposite has a kilim on the floor and a cushion that was the source of design for the others.

I wanted to use rows of straight stitch which are reminiscent of the original texture, but to do so meant some very odd calculations which were impossible to chart for this book. The solution was to use fabric pens and draw on the canvas. The fabric pens were used to define the areas of colour; they do not match the yarn shades. Begin sewing from the bottom and work in blocks of one colour or in rows like a knitting pattern, with each colour threaded on a separate needle ready to complete each row. Work as closely to the drawn shape as possible while maintaining the rows over three threads each time.

A coloured canvas saves much counting, even if the original drawing requires some time and ability; any irregularity in the pattern adds to the charm.

A white canvas was chosen to illustrate the drawing method (see page 118). A canvas closest in colour to the yarns used is generally advised.

The seat cushion (see page 119) measures 36 × 46 cm (14 × 18 in.) and is worked on an 18's mono canvas in three strands of Appletons crewel wool using one hank of each of the following colours: 151, 972, 124, 122, 311, 929 and 125. The cord used one hank each of 151, 311 and 929.

Adaptation: The pattern was copied from the previously completed needlepoint and when worked on a larger scale the design reproduced one corner only. Whatever scale the pattern is drawn at, it can still be worked over a small number of threads in straight lines.

The rectangular cushion measures 30 × 43 cm (12 × 17 in.) and was worked on a 14's mono canvas in Appletons tapestry wool using the following colours: 875, 992, 692, 965, 902, 931, 123, 153. The wool must not be pulled tight as it only just covers the canvas.

The collection of kilims was put together for an exhibition by Graham and Green in London, and evokes images of comfort and luxury.

Sequins and beads decorate the mirror frame
borders to indicate the sun on the sea, and the soft
shades of the shells opposite are captured by dyed
silk fabric yarn.

LARGE MIRROR FRAME

This free design is not charted

This design is based on the sea and seashells. I wanted to use the many shades achieved by hand-dyed silk yarn and chose a large area to display them. The mirror frame measures 84 × 64 cm (33 × 25 in.).

The white silk was sparsely dyed, giving some very pale areas among the deep blue, with some green and brown. The fabric was divided into strips and regrouped into colours, with wools, cottons, beads and sequins, some to tone and some to highlight. When a larger amount of one colour is required, as with the long, diagonal border stitches, complete the area before taking any of the colour for another part of the pattern.

The 18's mono canvas was mounted in as large an area of the floor frame as possible and the mirror frame shape was sketched out. The borders were worked and the sides completed with long straight stitches in a zig-zag and some lozenge shapes as shown in the chart to the right. Finer tent stitches were used to contrast with the larger textures and the beads and sequins were applied for fun – they are reminiscent of the sun on the sea.

Follow the instructions for making a mirror on page 54.

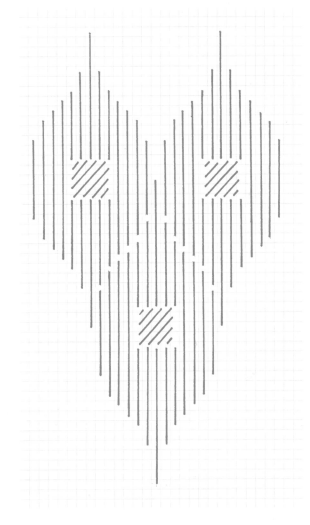

Shell colours are translated into the needlepoint design opposite.

123

DIAGONAL DESIGN

This design is not fully charted.

These designs are ideas for using stitches in diagonal bands with a velvet ribbon held in place by wool worked over it; the term for this is 'couching'. The chart overleaf shows some ideas that can be repeated or used in any order.

The zig-zag is a perennial design in needlepoint and the fabric shown is a new design which attracted me as it matched an area of the chair cover completed long before.

Decide on the area to be embroidered by thinking of it in terms of making your own fabric. Instead of pattern repeats that appear in woven and printed fabrics, the change of stitch or colour can create a unique piece.

Chart: See overleaf
Dimensions: To requirements
Canvas: 14's mono de luxe
Yarns: Start with two skeins of each colour. With the samples recorded on your project card, making additions to your requirements is simple. The colours used here were Appletons tapestry wool shades 201, 203, 935, 932, 127 and 714 and Anchor stranded cotton in the following colours: 811, 872, 883 and 339.
Needles: 18's tapestry needle
Extras: Velvet ribbon 9 mm wide
Notes: Couch the ribbon with a toning yarn.

Method

Start in the corner that suits you and work across. There are no rules as to whether to start in the widest point or the small corner of a square. The shape of the fabric template is completed in the same way, shaping the edges as necessary.

Adaptation: This idea can be used for making your own fabric for stools or chairs based on colours of existing furnishings, or a small panel for a cushion. It would appear prettier and less dramatic worked in pastel shades. To make an inset cushion see page 71.

UPHOLSTERY FABRIC

To make upholstery fabric it is necessary to cut an accurate template of the area in paper or fabric and mark it out on the canvas. If fabric is being replaced, use the old piece as a template, as it will include the shape of the folds and corners and show exactly the area to cover with embroidery. Remember that it is better to cover too much than too little, to avoid problems of bare canvas.

Once the area is marked, the chart overleaf can be worked as described.

When completed do not remove the piece from the frame until it is about to be used. After lightly pressing it on the wrong side, lay a soft towel over the work and roll both firmly round a cardboard tube and keep in a dry place. Present the needlepoint straight and smooth to an experienced upholsterer.

On the chair opposite, the velvet was of varying widths and a narrow velvet ribbon was considered most suitable as a trimming. The polyester velvet that was used has shown no signs of wear.

When designing your own 'fabric' for stools, chairs or footstools, an upholstery braid or fringing is often required to finish the piece. If you are not planning to make a matching cord from the yarns used in the needlepoint, select the braid or fringe *before* you start sewing.

Manufacturers have developed an amazing range of colourways but you will be fortunate

indeed to match your own blend of yarns, so do it in the way described on this page.

Selecting a braid

Take the project card with the colours and select the braid that is the closest. Take a sample of the 'close' braid back to the hundreds of embroidery shades available to you and match up one of the dominant braid colours to use in your needlepoint design. Then you will not be disappointed by failing to find a braid that will match exactly your completed work.

This method gives your work a totally co-ordinated look and displays a professional attention to detail.

Opposite: diagonal design chart.

WOODGRAIN BOLSTER

This design is not fully charted (see opposite and page 124)

The bolster design was prompted by the beautifully turned wooden bowl by Anthony Bryant, but the freely drawn pattern has been seen as being based on geological and meteorological sources as well as the original woodgrain.

The bowl suggested a design on the round, and although it is worked as a long panel, the interesting feature is that the whole design is never seen at one time.

The colours were taken from a remnant of woven silk that I had in store, knowing it would be useful one day!

Spalted beech bowl by Anthony Bryant.

Dimensions: 68 × 30 cm (27 × 12 in.)
Canvas: 14's mono de luxe 70 × 40 cm (31 × 16 in.)
Yarns: Quantities used for this size:
  5 × skeins DMC Medici wool
  7 × hanks Appletons tapestry wool
  11 × skeins DMC stranded cotton
  11 × skeins Anchor stranded cotton
The colours used here were so specific for the fabric that to number them is irrelevant, but choose about five colours and then shades of each from within that range. Do not work too tightly with six strands of cotton on a 14's canvas. If you are showing too much canvas, use eight or nine strands.

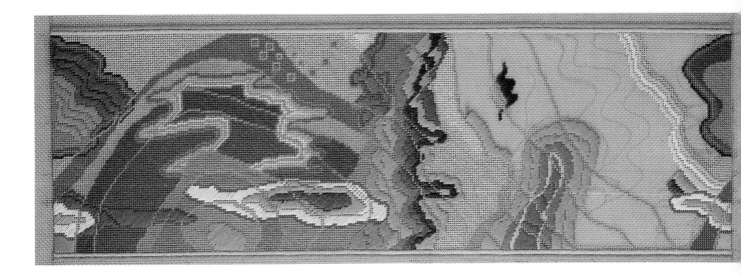

Needles: 18's, 20's tapestry
Extras: Fabric marker
Fabric, two pieces 72 × 40 cm (28 × 15½ in.)
Bolster pad 40 cm (16 in.) long
Cord to tie
Notes: This is a freehand drawing exercise. Find a source material that shows the grain of wood, leaf veins, map contours or a mineral pattern.

Method

Using the marker pen, draw lines to form the structure. Fill in areas with shades and patterns to suit. Remember that the two ends which will join round the circumference should link in some way.

The tent-stitched lines draw one pattern and another pattern is worked through them, like the cuts across the grain. The solid areas of wool contrast with smooth silky tent stitches in cotton. The sides that join with the fabric have narrow borders.

Making up

1 Trim the needlepoint with a canvas seam allowance of 1 cm (½ in.) all round.
2 Attach the fabric to the canvas by putting the long sides together, right sides facing.
3 Matching the fabric to the canvas edge for the seam allowance, machine together close to the embroidery.
4 Press fabric flat on the front.
5 Fold the total work in half, right sides together, giving areas of fabric, canvas and fabric. Tack carefully, to give accurate joins.
6 Machine together, in line with the embroidered edge. Trim fabric back to the 1 cm (½ in.) seam allowance and press seams flat.
7 Fold the fabric ends in to form a 10 cm (4 in.) hem, and hand stitch.
8 Turn inside out.
9 Ease the pad into place. Pull the fabric tightly over the ends and bind close to the pad with cord. The ends can be tucked in and a tassel or button fixed to cover the gathers but it leaves the bolster very difficult to pick up.

MINIATURE CUSHION

My interest in houses and their interior furnishings has not extended to the dolls' house although I am intrigued by the one-twelfth scale of each item. There are several specialist books on the subject of miniatures for the embroiderer, but I thought it would be fun to include something for the doll's home (see pages 132 and 133).

Chart: See below, produced in a large scale

Dimensions: 3.5 × 3 .5 cm (1⅛ × 1⅛ in.)

Canvas: 22's mono canvas 6 × 6 cm (2½ × 2½ in.)

Yarns: Lucy Coltman continuous space-dyed silk number 934

Eva Rosenstand and Clara Weaver fine cotton 122 and 140

Use two strands with all yarns.

Needles: 22's tapestry

Extras: Pieces of double-sided satin ribbon 1.5 mm wide × 5 cm (½ × 2 in.)

Backing fabric 5 × 5 cm (2 × 2 in.)

Soft fibre filling, polyester or wool

Sewing needle and matching thread

Notes: The chart is colour coded with the pattern colours, but any of the background areas, including some french knots, that are not labelled are worked with number 1.

Colour code

1 Lucy Coltman silk 934
2 ER/CW cotton 122
3 ER/CW cotton 140

ER/CW = Eva Rosenstand/Clara Weaver's stranded cotton

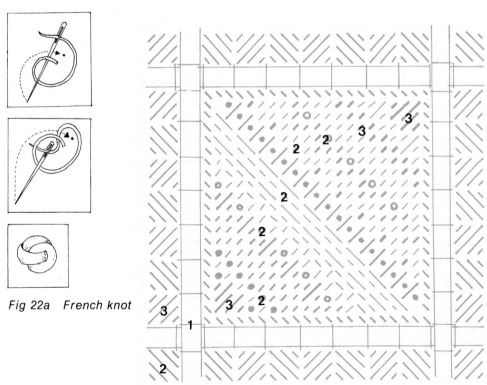

Fig 22a   French knot

131

Method

1 Measure and mark out the shape in the centre of the canvas. Use only as a guide.
2 Work diagonally from the central pattern to the corners.
3 Work the outside borders before couching the ribbons into place.

Making up

1 Cut the embroidery from the canvas with a 1 cm ($\frac{3}{8}$ in.) seam allowance.
2 There is no need to cut the corners, but make sure that all the turnings are neatly turned in and pressed, including the ribbons.
3 Repeat the process with the backing fabric, matching the shape to the front.
4 With the wrong sides facing, hand sew the edges together with fine stitches, securing the ribbon between the pieces.
5 Just before completing the fourth side, push sufficient filling inside to suit the purpose.

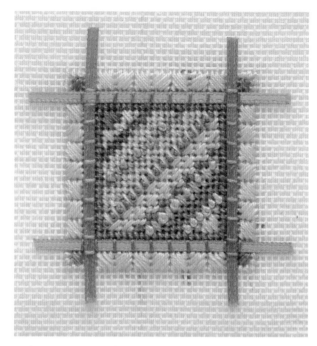

Adaptation: The chart can be used with any size canvas and suitable yarns. Mixing wool with cotton and replacing the french knots with beads would make an interesting pincushion worked on an 18's canvas.

Dolls house drawing room with needlepoint cushions

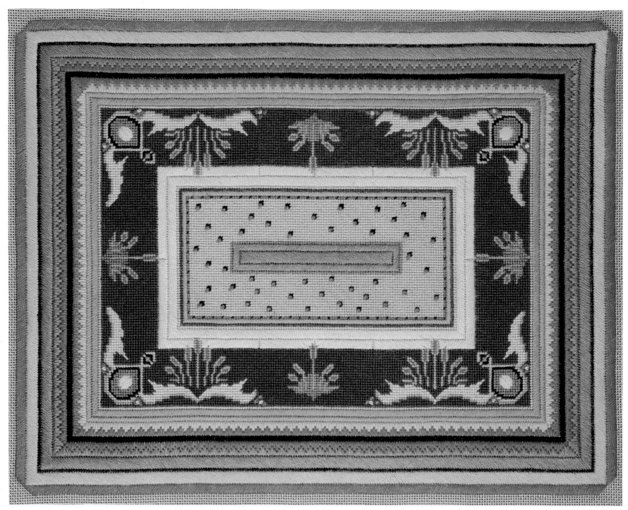

This piece was worked on a 14's mono de luxe
canvas and the embroidered area measures
34 × 44 cm (13½ × 17½ in). The colours are
Appletons tapestry wool numbers 298, 224, 221,
692, 952, 955, 332 and 292.

COMPOSITE CUSHION

This design idea is not fully charted.

Charts: See pages 28, 33, and 37

This pattern is an amalgam of charted pieces already seen in the book. The cushion is intended to rest on a stool with the corners tied to the ornamental sides, so the corners have been angled to allow the braid to be attached.

To make a cushion for a specific seat, make a paper template to fit which can be used to mark the area on the canvas and as a pattern for the backing. Remember that the outline is only a guide – the stitch line can be adjusted after accurately marking up. The centre thread in each direction has to be marked for this pattern and, to help with the borders, a line passing through the holes from each corner will mark the exact turning point.

Figure 23a indicates the different charts used but you will have to contribute some thought to your layout to fit the situation for your cushion. Work the borders and adjust the central area.

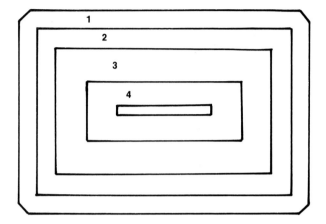

Fig 23a

1 Diagonal satin stitch borders
2 Chart Page 33
3 Chart Page 28
4 Chart Page 37

PHOTOCOPYING AND DESIGNS

Photocopiers are items of modern technology that we have accepted into our lives. There are plenty of opportunities to use them, as machines are available for use in shops and libraries.

There are copyright laws worldwide and it is most important not to abuse them. Authors, designers and composers are powerless against daily infringement. However, think of the copier as another tool to use with the books you have purchased – extract a pattern for easy carrying, or enlarge sections for clarity. Such extraction is permissible as long as the photocopies are solely for your own use and are not sold, used to produce kits or run classes.

Make patterns with the photocopier. If a photocopy is made of a piece of patterned fabric, the outline on paper is much clearer and makes the transfer to canvas much easier. To embroider part of a fabric design into your project co-ordinates your work with the existing interior furnishings.

Some people are already skilled in manipulating the copier as a design machine to produce an exciting art form, but here is a suggestion for a modest start.

Take a section of canvas. Enlarge it to the maximum capacity of a simple machine and overlap the photocopies so they form a pattern. The woven threads get distorted and a pattern emerges of small pillows. I have selected some threads and beads, and the photograph opposite shows my test sample. For this I used glass beads, sequins, Neon Rays needlepoint ribbon NO6, ultra-suede U82 and Eva Rosenstand and Clara Weaver stranded cotton 108, 125 and 110.

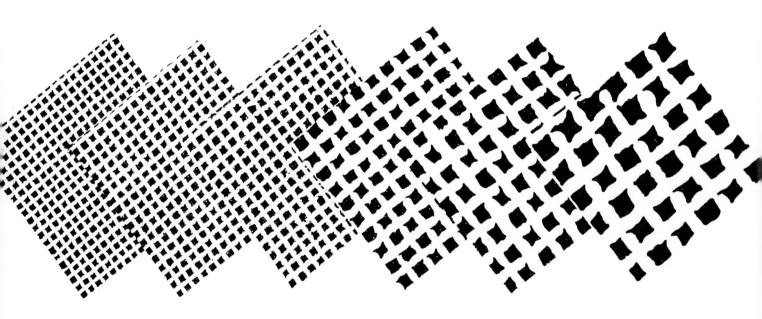

This piece of needlepoint has been created using
the photocopier as a design tool. Glass beads and
sequins enhance the pattern.

BIBLIOGRAPHY

Helena Barrett and John Phillips, *Suburban Style*, MacDonald Orbis 1987

Geoffrey Beard, *Craftsmen and Interior Decoration in England 1660–1820*, John Bartholomew and Son 1988

Victoria Ebin, *The Body Decorated*, Thames and Hudson 1979

William Fagg, *Yoruba Beadwork*, Lund Humphries 1980

Mary Gilliatt, *English Country Style*, MacDonald Orbis 1986

Merle Good, *Who are the Amish?*, Good Books, Pennsylvania 1985

Malcolm Haslam, *Art Deco*, MacDonald Orbis 1987

Johannes Kalter, *The Arts and Crafts of Turkestan*, Thames and Hudson 1984

Jane Lemon, *Embroidered Boxes*, B.T. Batsford 1989

Jan Messent, *The Embroiderer's Workbook*, B.T. Batsford 1989

Rozsika Parker, *The Subversive Stitch*, The Women's Press 1984

The Quilt Digest, Quilt Digest Press San Francisco 1986

Mary Rhodes, *Dictionary of Canvas Work Stitches*, B.T. Batsford 1980

Jane Tiller, *Regency and Victorian Crafts*, Ward Lock 1969

V&A. Colour Books, Webb and Bower 1986–7

Raymond Williams, *Culture and Society*, Hogarth Press 1987

SUPPLIERS

Good embroidery shops
Hepatica
82a Water Lane
Wilmslow
Cheshire

Russells
30 Castle Street
Carlisle
Cumbria

Christine Riley
53 Barclay Street
Stonehaven
Kincardineshire

Campden Needlecraft
High Street
Chipping Campden
Gloucestershire

The Tapestry Centre
42 West Street
Alresford
Hampshire

Canada

Dick and Jane
2352 West 41st Avenue
Vancouver
British Columbia

New Zealand

The Embroiderer
142a Hinemoa Street
Birkenhead
Auckland

Broomfields
16 Merivale Mall
Christchurch

Both these shops stock the New Zealand mohair required for the stool top.

USA

Family Arts Exchange
711 East Palo Verde Drive
Phoenix
Arizona

The Needle Point
123 South Hemlock
Ecola Square
Cannon Beach
OR 97110

Janna's Needle Art
5091 N. Fresno 117
Fresno CA 93710

Needlepoint
7608 Fay Avenue
La Jolla CA 92037

My apologies if this appears an inadequate list. These are the shops that have impressed me with their extensive ranges and where I have been tempted with new threads, some of which are used in the book. There are of course many more that I have not visited. They are all generous with their time and advice, but if enquiring by post it is only fair to enclose a stamped addressed envelope.

Specialist stockists
Beads and sequins:
Theatrical Supplies
56 Welford Road
Leicester

Shaker boxes in photographs from:
Frye's Measure Mill
Wilton
New Hampshire 03086
USA

In England there is:
The Shaker Shop
25 Harcourt Street
London W1

Rugs featured in photograph were from:
Quinns Gallery
Pen Street
Boston
Lincolnshire

The kilim cushion used as a design source was from:
The Gordon Reece Gallery
Finkle Street
Knaresborough
North Yorkshire

Rugs and interesting objects for the home:
Graham and Green
4 & 7 Elgin Crescent
London W11

Handcrafted chatelaine tools and antiques or collectables:
Log Cabin Needleworks
PO Box 1705
Coarsegold
California 93614

Eva Rosenstand and Clara Weaver cottons; information USA:
Merry Cox
PO Box 185
Clovis
California 93613

Information and enquiries about the New Zealand mohair and wool:
Strand Natural Fibres
PO Box 13–138
Wellington
New Zealand

Antique textiles and tassels:
The Green Room
Framlingham
Suffolk

Chart paper:
H.W. Peel & Co.
Norwester House
Fairway Drive
Greenford
Middlesex UB6 8PW

Dolls' house furniture:
Craftys
54A Fore Street
St Ives
Cornwall

Terracotta urns and large pots:
Tydd Pottery
Pinchbeck
Spalding
Lincolnshire

Wooden bowls:
Anthony Bryant
Helston
Cornwall

INDEX